NALA AND DAMAYANTI

AND OTHER POEMS

NALA AND DAMAYANTI

AND OTHER POEMS

TRANSLATED FROM THE SANSCRIT INTO ENGLISH VERSE, WITH MYTHOLOGICAL AND CRITICAL NOTES.

BY THE

REV. HENRY HART MILMAN, M.A.

GYAN

Published by

Gyan Publishing House
5, Ansari Road
Daryaganj, New Delhi-110002
Phone: 011-47034999, 9811692060
E-mail: books@gyanbooks.com

Distribution Network
gyanbooks.com
India, USA, Canada, UK, Australia, France

ISBN: 978-81-212-7182-0 (PB)
First Published, 1835

2nd Impression 2024

Printed at: Gyan Press, Delhi.

NALA AND DAMAYANTI AND OTHER POEMS
Translator: HENRY HART MILMAN

NALA AND DAMAYANTI

AND OTHER POEMS

TRANSLATED FROM THE SANSCRIT INTO ENGLISH VERSE, WITH MYTHOLOGICAL AND CRITICAL NOTES.

BY THE

REV. HENRY HART MILMAN, M. A.

PREBENDARY OF WESTMINSTER; MINISTER OF ST. MARGARET'S; AND LATE PROFESSOR OF POETRY IN THE UNIVERSITY OF OXFORD.

OXFORD: D. A. TALBOYS.

M DCCC XXXV.

TO MY MOTHER,

TO WHOM THESE TRANSLATIONS HAVE AFFORDED
MUCH PLEASURE,

AND TO WHOM, AT HER ADVANCED AGE,
TO HAVE AFFORDED PLEASURE,

IS THE MOST GRATIFYING REWARD OF LITERARY
LABOUR,

THIS VOLUME IS INSCRIBED,

BY HER AFFECTIONATE SON.

CONTENTS:

PREFACE.

Those friends who have taken an interest in my literary productions may feel some surprise at my appearance in the character of a translator of Sanscrit poetry. To those, and indeed to all who may take up the present volume, I owe some explanation of my pretensions as a faithful interpreter of my original text. Those pretensions are very humble; and I can unfeignedly say, that if the field had been likely to be occupied by others, who might unite poetical powers with a profound knowledge of the sacred language of India, I should have withdrawn at once from the competition. But, in fact, in this country the students of oriental literature, endowed with a taste and feeling for poetry, are so few in number, that any attempt to make known the peculiar character of those remarkable works, the old mythological epics of India, may be received with indulgence by all who are interested in the history of poetry. Mr. Wilson alone, since Sir W. Jones, has united a poetical genius with deep Sanscrit scholarship; but he has in general preferred the later and more polished period—that of Kalidasa and the dramatists—to the ruder, yet in my opinion, not less curious and poetical strains of the older epic bards.

A brief account of the manner in which I became engaged in these studies, will best explain the extent of my proficiency. During the two last years in which I held the office of Professor of Poetry in the University of Oxford, having exhausted the subject which I had chosen for my terminal course, I was at a loss for some materials for the few remaining lectures before my office should expire. I had been led by the ardent curiosity, which I have ever felt to acquire some knowledge of the poetry of all ages and nations—to examine some of the publications of French and German, as well as English scholars, on the subject of Indian poetry; chiefly those of the Schlegels, of Bopp, and of De Chezy. I was struck with the singularity and captivated by the extreme beauty, as it appeared to me, of some of the extracts, especially those from the great epic poems, the Mahabharat and the Ramayana, in their Homeric simplicity so totally opposite to the ordinary notions entertained of all eastern poetry. I was induced to attempt, without any instruction, and with the few elementary works which could be procured, the Grammars of Wilkins and Bopp, the Glossaries of Bopp and Rosen (Mr. Wilson's Dictionary was then out of print and could not be purchased), to obtain some knowledge of this wonderful and mysterious language. The study grew upon me, and would have been pursued with more ardour, perhaps with more success, but for the constant interruption of more imperative professional and literary avocations. In itself the Sanscrit is an inexhaustible subject of interest; in its grammatical structure more regular, artificial, and copious than the most perfect of the western languages; in its origin, the parent from which the older Greek, the Latin and the Teutonic tongues seem to branch out and develope themselves upon distinct and discernible principles.

I ventured to communicate to the Members of the University who attended my lectures, my discoveries, as it were, in the unknown region of Indian poetry, and to introduce translations of such passages as appeared to me of peculiar singularity or beauty. Though I was still moving in the leading-strings of my learned guides, I had obtained sufficient acquaintance with the language to compare their interpretations with the original text. I afterwards embodied some parts of my lectures in an article in the Quarterly Review, in order to contribute as far as was in my power to open this new and almost untrodden field of literature to the English reader.

Still I should not have presumed to form these translations into a separate work, nor acceded to the proposal of the publisher of the present volume, who has himself deserved so well of the students of oriental lore by his excellent translation, or rather recomposition of Adelung's "Historical Sketch of Sanscrit Literature," but for the encouragement and assistance of Mr. Wilson, now, the University may be proud to say, the Boden Professor of Sanscrit at Oxford. To his most friendly care in revising these sheets, I owe the correction of many errors; and Sanscrit scholars will find in the notes some observations on the text, which will contribute to elucidate the poem of Nala. Under the sanction of Mr. Wilson's revision, I may venture to hope that the translation is, at least, an accurate version of the original; and I cannot too strongly express my gratitude for the labour which Mr. Wilson has been so kind as to expend on my imperfect and unpretending work.

The versification, or rather the metrical system, which I have adopted, is an experiment, how far a successful one must be judged by others. The original verse in which the vast epics of Vyasa and Valmiki are composed is called the Sloka, which is thus described by Schlegel in his Indische Bibliothek, p. 36: "The oldest, most simple, and most generally adopted measure is the Sloka; a distich of two sixteen syllable-lines, divided at the eighth syllable." According to our prosodial marks, the following is the scheme :—

⏓ ⏓ ⏓ ⏓ | ˘ ¯ ¯ ⏒ | ⏓ ⏓ ⏓ ⏓ | ˘ ¯ ˘ ⏒
⏓ ⏓ ⏓ ⏓ | ⏓ ¯ ¯ ⏒ | ⏓ ⏓ ⏓ ⏓ | ˘ ¯ ˘ ⏓

The first four syllables are bound by no rule; the second half, on the contrary, is unalterably fixed, excepting that the last syllable has the common licence of termination. In the second half verse, I do not remember a single instance of deviation from this, though sometimes, but very seldom, the first half verse ends with another quadrisyllable foot. The reader who is curious on the subject, may compare Mr. Colebrooke's elaborate essays on Sanscrit poetry, Kosegarten's preface to his Translation of Nala, and Bopp's preface to his Translation of Selections from the Mahabharat.

In the first translations which I attempted, a few passages from the Bhagavat-Gíta, I adhered as nearly as possible to the measure of the original; in the Nala, in order to give the narrative a more easy and trochaic flow, I omitted one syllable, and in some degree changed the structure of the verse.

July 1835.

NALA AND DAMAYANTI.

The episode of Nala is extracted from the Vanaparvam, the third part of the Mahábhárata, the great Indian poem, which contains 100,000 slokas, or distichs. The sage, Vrihadasva, relates the story of Nala to king Yudhishthira, in order to console him under the miseries to which he was exposed by bad success in play. By the terms of the gaming transaction, in which he was worsted by Sakuni, who threw the dice for Duryodhana, he was condemned to wander with his brothers for twelve years in the forest. The adventures of Nala showed how that king, having been in the same manner unfortunate with the dice, had suffered still greater toil and misery, and had at length recovered his kingdom and his wife. The popularity of this fable with the natives, is sufficiently proved by the numerous poetic versions of the story. The Nalodaya, a poem ascribed to Kalidas, should first be mentioned. A new edition of this work has been recently published by Ferdinand Benary; we have a notice of it in the Quarterly Review: it seems to bear the same relation to the simple and national episode of the Mahábhárat, as the seicentesti of Italy to Dante or Ariosto, or Gongora to the poem of the Cid. Another poem called Naishadha, in twenty-two books, does not complete the story, but only carries it as far as the fifteenth book. There is a Tamulic version of the same story, translated by Kindersley, in his specimens of Hindu Literature. The third book of the poem of Srïharsha, containing 135 slokas, is entirely occupied with the conversation between Damayanti and the swans (the geese), in which the birds to excite her love, dwell with diffuse eloquence on the praises of Nala.

NALA AND DAMAYANTI.

BOOK I.

LIVED of yore, a raja, Nala,—Virasena's mighty son,
Gifted he with every virtue,—beauteous, skilled in taming steeds:
Head of all the kings of mortals—like the monarch of the gods,
Over, over all exalted—in his splendour like the sun:
Holy, deep-read in the Vedas—in Nishadha lord of earth;
Loving dice, of truth unblemished—chieftain of a mighty host.
The admired of noble women—generous, with each sense subdued.
Guardian of the state; of archers—best, a present Manu he.
So there dwelt in high Vidarbha—Bhima, terrible in strength,
With all virtues blest, but childless—long for children had he pined.
Many an holy act, on offspring—still intent, had he performed.
To his court there came a Brahmin,—Damana the seer was named.
Him the child-desiring Bhima—in all duties skilled, received,
Feasted with his royal consort—in his hospitable hall.
Pleased on him the grateful Daman,—and his queen a boon bestowed,
One sweet girl, the pearl of maidens—and three fair and noble sons.
Damayanti, Dama Dánta—and illustrious Damana,
Richly gifted with all virtues—mighty, fearful in their might.
Damayanti with her beauty—with her brilliance, brightness, grace,
Through the worlds unrivalled glory—won the slender-waisted maid.
Her, arrived at bloom of beauty,—sate a hundred slaves around,
And a hundred virgin handmaids—as around great Indra's queen.

B 2

In her court shone Bhima's daughter—decked with every ornament,
Mid her handmaids, like the lightning—shone she with her faultless form;
Like the long-eyed queen of beauty—without rival, without peer.
Never mid the gods immortal—never mid the Yaksha race,
Nor 'mong men was maid so lovely—ever heard of, ever seen,
As the soul-disturbing maiden—that disturbed the souls of gods.
Nala too, 'mong kings the tiger—peerless among earthly men,
Like Kandarpa in his beauty—like that bright-embodied God.
All around Vidarbha's princess—praised they Nala in their joy.
Ever praised they Damayanti—round Nishadha's noble king.
Hearing so each others virtues—all unseen they 'gan to love.
Thus of each, O son of Kunti,—the deep silent passion grew.
Nala, in his heart impatient—longer that deep love to bear,
To the grove, in secret, wandered—by the palace' inmost court.
There the swans he saw disporting—with their wings bedropped with gold:
Through the grove thus lightly moving—one of these bright birds he caught.
But the bird, in human language—thus the wondering king addressed:
" Slay me not, O gentle monarch!—I will do thee service true;
" So in Damayanti's presence—will I praise Nishadha's king,
" Never after shall the maiden—think of mortal man but thee."
Thus addressed, at once the monarch—let the bright-winged bird depart.
Flew away the swans rejoicing—to Vidarbha straight they flew;
To Vidharba's stately city:—there by Damayanti's feet,
Down with drooping plumes they settled—and she gazed upon the flock,
Wondering at their forms so graceful—where amid her maids she sate.
Sportively began the damsels—all around to chase the birds;
Scattering flew the swans before them—all about the lovely grove.
Lightly ran the nimble maidens,—every one her bird pursued;

But the swan that through the forest—gentle Damayanti chased,
Suddenly, in human language—spake to Damayanti thus.—
"Damayanti, in Nishadha—Nala dwells, the noble king—
"Like the Aswinas in beauty,—peerless among men is he.
"O incomparable princess—to this hero wert thou wed,
"Noble birth and perfect beauty—not unworthy fruit had borne.
"Gods, Gandharvas, men, the Serpents,—and the Rákshasas we've seen,
"All we've seen—of noble Nala—never have we seen the peer.
"Pearl art thou among all women—Nala is the pride of men.
"If the peerless wed the peerless—blessed must the union be."
When the bird thus strangely speaking—gentle Damayanti heard,
Answered thus the wondering maiden—"Thus to Nala, speak thou too."
"Be it so," replied the egg-born—to Vidarbha's beauteous maid.
Home then flew he to Nishadha—and to Nala told it all.

BOOK II.

Damayanti, ever after—she the swan's sweet speech had heard—
With herself she dwelt no longer—all herself with Nala dwelt.
Lost in thought she sate dejected—pale her melancholy cheek,
Damayanti sate and yielded—all her soul to sighs of grief.
Upward gazing, meditative—with a wild distracted look,
Wan was all her soft complexion—and with passion heart-possessed,
Nor in sleep nor gentle converse—nor in banquets found she joy;
Night nor day she could not slumber—Woe! oh woe! she wept and said.
Her no longer her own mistress—from her looks, her gesture, knew
Damayanti's virgin handmaids—to Vidarbha's monarch they
Told how pined his gentle daughter—for the sovereign of men.
This from Damayanti's maidens—when the royal Bhima heard,
In his mind he gravely pondered—for his child what best were done.
"Wherefore is my gentle daughter—from herself in mind estranged?"
When the lord of earth his daughter—saw in blooming youth mature,
Knew he for the Swayembara—Damayanti's time was come.
Straight the lord of many peasants—summoned all the chiefs of earth,
"Come ye to the Swayembara—all ye heroes of the world!"
Damayanti's Swayembara—soon as heard the kings of men,
All obeyed king Bhima's summons—all to Bhima's court drew near;
Elephants, and steeds, and chariots—swarmed along the sounding land;
All with rich and various garlands—with his stately army each—
All the lofty-minded rajas—Bhima with the arm of strength,
As beseemed, received with honour—on their thrones of state they sate.

At this very hour the wisest—of the sages, the divine,
Moving in their might ascended—up from earth to Indra's world.
Great in holiness and wisdom—Narada and Parvata
Honoured entered they the palace—of the monarch of the gods.
Them salutes the cloud-compeller—of their everlasting weal,
Of their weal the worlds pervading—courteous asks the immortal lord.

NARADA *spake.*

Well it fares with us, Immortal—in our weal the world partakes—
In the world, O cloud-compeller—well it fares with all her kings.

VRIHADASVA *spake.*

He that Bali slew and Vritra—asked of Narada again—
All earth's just and righteous rulers—reckless of their lives in fight—
Who the shafts' descending death-blow—meet with unaverted eye—
Theirs this everlasting kingdom—even as Kamadhuk is mine.
Where are they, the Kshetriya heroes?—wherefore see I not approach
All the earth's majestic guardians—all mine ever-honoured guests.
Thus addressed by holy Sakra—Narada replied and said:
"Hear me now, O cloud-compeller—why earth's kings appear not here.
"Of Vidarbha's king the daughter—Damayanti, the renowned;
"Through the earth the loveliest women—in her beauty she transcends—
"Soon she holds her Swayembara—soon her lord the maid will choose.
"Thither all the kings are hastening—thither all the sons of kings.
"Suitors for her hand the rajas—her of all the world the pearl,
"O thou mighty giant slayer!—one and all approach to woo."
As they spake, the world-protectors—with the god of fire drew near;
Of the immortals all, the highest—stood before the king of gods.

As they all stood silent hearing—Narada's majestic speech,
All exclaimed in sudden rapture—thither we likewise will go;
All the immortals on the instant,—with their chariots, with their hosts,
Hastened down towards Vidarbha—where the lords of earth were met.
Nala, too, no sooner heard he—of that concourse of the kings,
Set he forth, with soul all sanguine—full of Damayanti's love.
Saw the gods, king Nala standing—on the surface of the earth;
Standing in transcendant beauty--equal to the god of love.
Him beheld the world's high guardians—in his radiance like the sun;
Each arrested stood and silent—at his peerless form amazed.
All their chariots the celestials—in the midway air have checked,
Through the blue air then descending—they Nishadha's king address.
Ho! what, ho! Nishadha's monarch—Nala, king, for truth renowned;
Do our bidding, bear our message—O, most excellent of men.

BOOK III.

Nala made his solemn promise,—"all your bidding will I do;"
Then with folded hands adoring—humbly of their will enquired.
"Who are ye? to whom must Nala—as your welcome herald go?
"What is my commanded service?—tell me, mighty gods, the truth."
Spake the sovereign of Nishadha—Indra answered thus and said:—
"Know us, the Immortals, hither—come for Damayanti's love.
"Indra I, and yon is Agni,—and the king of waters there—
"Slayer he of mortal bodies,—Yama, too, is here, O king!
"Thou, O Nala, of our coming,—must to Damayanti tell:
"Thee to see, the world's dread guardians—Indra and the rest came down,
"Indra, Agni, Varun, Yama,—each to seek thine hand are come.
"One of these celestial beings,—choose, O maiden, for thy lord."
Nala, thus addressed by Indra—with his folded hands replied:
"Thus with one accord commanding—on this mission send not me.
"How can man, himself enamoured—for another plead his cause?
"Spare me then, ye gods, in mercy—this unwelcome service, spare."

The Gods *spake.*

"I will do your bidding freely—thus thou'st said, Nishadha's king;
"Wilt thou now belie thy promise?—Nala, go, nor more delay."
By the gods adjured so sternly—thus rejoined Nishadha's king—
"Strictly guarded is yon palace—how may I find entrance there?"
"Thou shalt enter;" thus did Indra—to the unwilling king reply.
In the bower of Damayanti—as they spake, king Nala stood.
There he saw Vidarbha's maiden—girt with all her virgin bands;

C

In her glowing beauty shining—all excelling in her form;
Every limb in smooth proportion—slender waist and lovely eyes;
Even the moon's soft gleam disdaining—in her own o'erpowering light.
As he gazed, his love grew warmer—to the softly smiling maid,
Yet to keep his truth, his duty—all his passion he suppressed.
Then Nishadha's king beholding—all those maids with beauteous limbs
From their seats sprang up in wonder—at his matchless form amazed.
In their rapture to king Nala—all admiring, homage paid;
Yet, not venturing to accost him,—in their secret souls adored.
"Oh the beauty! oh the splendour!—oh the mighty hero's strength!
"Who is he, or God, or Yaksha—or Gandharba may he be."
Not one single word to utter,—dared that fair-limbed maiden band;
All struck dumb before his beauty—in their bashful silence stood.
Smiling, first, upon the monarch—as on her he gently smiled,
Damayanti, in her wonder—to the hero Nala spake:—
"Who art thou of form so beauteous—thou that wakenest all my love;
"Cam'st thou here like an immortal—I would know thee, sinless chief.
"How hast entered in our palace?—how hast entered all unseen?
"Watchful are our chamber wardens—stern the mandate of the king."
By the maiden of Vidarbha—Nala thus addressed, replied:—
"Know, O loveliest, I am Nala—here the messenger of gods,
"Gods desirous to possess thee;—one of these, the lord of heaven
"Indra, Agni, Varun, Yama,—choose thou, princess, for thy lord.
"Through their power, their power almighty—I have entered here unseen;
"As I entered in thy chamber—none hath seen, and none might stay.
"This, the object of my mission,—fairest, from the highest gods,
"Thou hast heard me, noble princess—even as thou wilt, decide."

BOOK IV.

To the gods performed her homage—smiled she, and to Nala spake:—
" Pledge to me thy faith, O raja—how that faith, may I requite?
" I myself, and whatsoever—in the world I have, is thine
" In full trust is thine—O grant me—in thy turn thy love, O king!
" 'Tis the swan's enamouring language—that hath kindled all my soul.
" Only for thy sake, O hero—are the assembled rajas met.
" But if thou mine homage scornest—scornest me, all honoured king,
" Poison for thy sake, fire, water,—the vile noose will I endure."
So, when spake Vidarbha's maiden—Nala answered thus, and said:—
" With the world's dread guardians present—wilt thou mortal husband choose?
" We with them, the world's creators—with these mighty lords compared,
" Lowlier than the dust they tread on—raise to them thy loftier mind.
" Man the gods displeasing, hastens—to inevitable death—
" Fair limbed! from that fate preserve me—choose the all excelling gods.
" Robes by earthly dust unsullied—crowns of amaranthine flowers,
" Every bright celestial glory—wedded to the gods, enjoy.
" He, who all the world compressing—with devouring might consumes,
" Sovereign of the gods, Hutása,—where is she who would not wed?
" He, in awe of whose dread sceptre—all the assembled hosts of men,
" Cultivate eternal justice—where is she who would not wed?
" Him the all-righteous, lofty minded,—slayer of the infernal host,
" Of all gods, the mighty monarch,—who is she that would not wed?
" Nor let trembling doubt arrest thee—in thy mind if thou couldst choose.
" Varuna, amongst earth's guardians,—hear the language of a friend."
To the sovereign of Nishadha—Damayanti spake, and said,

And her eyes grew dim with moisture—flowing from her inward grief:—
"To the gods, to all, my homage—king of earth, I humbly pay;
"Yet thee only, thee, my husband—may I choose, Be this my vow!"
Answered he the trembling maiden—as with folded hands she stood,
"Bound upon this solemn mission—mine own cause how dare I urge.
"Plighted by a sacred promise—to the everlasting gods;
"Thus engaged to plead for others—for myself I may not plead.
"This my duty; yet hereafter—come I on my own behalf,
"Then I'll plead mine own cause boldly—weigh it, beauteous, in thy thought."
Damayanti smiled serenely,—and with tear-impeded speech,
Uttered brokenly and slowly—thus to royal Nala spake:—
"Yet I see a way of refuge—'tis a blameless way, O king;
"Whence no sin to thee, O raja,—may by any chance arise.
"Thou, O noblest of all mortals—and the gods by Indra led,
"Come and enter in together—where the Swayembara meets;
"Then will I, before the presence—of the guardians of the world,
"Name thee, lord of men! my husband—nor to thee may blame accrue."
By the maiden of Vidarbha—royal Nala thus addressed,
Back again returned, where waited—eager, the expecting gods.
Him, the guardians of the world, the mighty—ere he yet drew near, beheld,
Him they saw, and bade him instant—all his tidings to unfold—
"Was she seen of thee, O monarch—Damayanti with soft smile?
"Spake she of us all? what said she?—tell, O blameless lord of earth."

NALA *spake.*

To the bower of Damayanti—on your solemn mission sent,
Entered I the lofty portal—by the aged warders watched;
Mortal eye might not behold me—there as swift I entered in;

None save that fair raja's daughter—through your all prevailing power.
And her virgin handmaids, saw I—and by them in turn was seen;
And they all in mute amazement—gazed upon me as I stood.
I described your godlike presence—but the maid with beauteous face
Chooses me, bereft of reason—O most excellent of gods!
Thus she spake, that maiden princess,—"Let the gods together come,
"Come with thee, Oh king of mortals,—where the Swayembara meets;
"There will I, before their presence—choose thee, raja, for my lord.
"So to thee, O strong armed warrior—may no blame, no fault ensue."
Thus it was, even as I tell you—word for word did it befall.
Plainly have I spoke, the judgment—rests with you, of gods the chief!

BOOK V.

CAME the day of happy omen—moonday meet, and moment apt;
Bhima to the Swayembara—summoned all the lords of earth.
One and all, upon the instant—rose th' enamoured lords of earth,
Suitors all to Damayanti—in their loving haste they came.
They, the court with golden columns—rich, and glittering portal arch,
Like the lions on the mountains—entered they the hall of state.
There the lords of earth were seated—each upon his several throne;
All their fragrant garlands wearing—all with pendant ear-gems rich.
Arms were seen robust and vigorous—as the ponderous battle mace,
Some like the five-headed serpents—delicate in shape and hue:
With bright locks profuse and flowing—fine formed nose, and eye and brow,
Shone the faces of the rajas—like the radiant stars in heaven.
As with serpents, Bhogavati—the wide hall was full of kings;
As the mountain caves with tigers—with the tiger-warriors full.
Damayanti in her beauty—entered on that stately scene,
With her dazzling light entrancing—every eye and every soul.
O'er her lovely person gliding—all the eyes of those proud kings;
There were fixed, there moveless rested—as they gazed upon the maid.
Then as they proclaimed the rajas—(by his name was each proclaimed)
In dismay saw Bhima's daughter—five in garb, in form the same.
On those forms, all undistinguished—each from each, she stood and gazed.
In her doubt Vidarbha's princess—Nala's form might not discern,
Whichsoe'er the form she gazed on—him her Nala, him she thought.
She within her secret spirit—deeply pondering, stood and thought:
" How shall I the gods distinguish?—royal Nala how discern?"

Pondering thus Vidarbha's maiden—in the anguish of her heart—
Th' attributes of the immortals—sought, as heard of yore, to see.
"Th' attributes of each celestial—that our aged sires describe,
"As on earth they stand before me—not of one may I discern."
Long she pondered in her silence—and again, again she thought.
To the gods, her only refuge—turned she at this trying hour.
With her voice and with her spirit—she her humble homage paid.
Folding both her hands and trembling—to the gods the maiden spake:
"As when heard the swan's sweet language—chose I then Nishadha's king,
"By this truth I here adjure ye—oh, ye gods, reveal my lord;
"As in word or thought I swerve not—from my faith, all-knowing powers,
"By this truth I here adjure ye—oh, ye gods, reveal my lord.
"As the gods themselves have destined—for my lord Nishadha's king;
"By this truth I here adjure ye—oh, ye gods, my lord reveal.
"As my vow, so pledged to Nala—holily must be maintained,
"By this truth I here adjure ye—oh, ye gods, my lord reveal.
"Each the form divine assume ye—earth's protectors, mighty lords;
"So shall I discern my Nala—I shall know the king of men."

As they heard sad Damayanti—uttering thus her piteous prayer,
At her high resolve they wonder—steadfast truth and fervent love,
Holiness of soul, and wisdom—to her lord her constant faith.
As she prayed, the gods obedient—stood with attributes revealed:
With unmoistened skins the Immortals—saw she, and with moveless eyes;
Fresh their dust-unsullied garlands—hovered they, nor touched the earth.
On his shadow garland-drooping—soiled with dust and moist with sweat,
On the earth Nishadha's monarch—stood confessed, with twinkling eyes;
On the gods an instant gazed she—then upon the king of men;
And of right king Bhima's daughter—named Nishadha's king her lord.

Modestly the large-eyed maiden—lifted up his garment's hem,
Round his shoulders threw she lightly—the bright zone of radiant flowers;
So she chose him for her husband—Nala, that high-hearted maid.
Then alas! alas! burst wildly,—from that conclave of the kings,
And "well done, well done," as loudly—from the gods and sages broke;
All in their extatic wonder—glorified Nishadha's king.
Then to royal Damayanti—Virasena's kingly son,
To that slender waisted damsel—spake he comfort in his joy;
" Since thou'st own'd me for thine husband—in the presence of the gods,
" For thy faithful consort know me—aye delighting in thy words.
" While this spirit fills this body—maiden with the smile serene!
" Thine am I, so long thine only—this the solemn truth I vow."
Thus he gladdened Damayanti—with the assurance of his faith;
And the happy pair devoutly—worshipped then the present gods.
Chosen thus Nishadha's monarch—the bright guardians of the world,
In their gladness all on Nala—eight transcendant gifts bestowed;
To discern the visible godhead—in the sacrifice, a gait
Firm and noble, Sachi's husband—Indra to king Nala gave.
Agni gave his own bright presence—whensoe'er the monarch called.
All the worlds instinct with splendour—through his power Hutasa gave.
Subtle taste in food gave Yama—and in virtue eminence;
Varun gave obedient water—to be present at his call;
Garlands too of matchless fragrance;—each his double blessing gave.
Thus bestowed their gracious favours—to the heavens the gods returned;
And the rajas, who with wonder—Nala's marriage saw confirmed
With the gentle Damayanti—as they came, in joy returned.
Thus the kings of earth departed;—Bhima in his joy and pride,
Solemnized the stately bridals—of the maiden and the king.

Fitting time when there he'd sojourned,—best of men, Nishadha's king;
Courteous parting with king Bhima—to his native city went.
Having gained the pearl of women—the majestic lord of earth
Lived in bliss, as with his Sachi,—he that those old giants slew.
In his joy the elated monarch—shining radiant as the sun,
Ruled the subjects of his kingdom—with a just and equal sway.
Of the horse the famous offering—like Nahucha's mighty son,
Every sacrifice performed he—with rich gifts to holy men.
And full oft in flowering gardens—and delicious shady groves,
Like a god, the royal Nala—took with Damayanti joy.
So begat from Damayanti—Nala, of heroic soul,
Indrasena one fair daughter—Indrasen one beauteous son.
Thus in sacrifice and pleasance—took his joy the king of men,
So the earth with riches teeming—ruled the sovereign of the earth.

BOOK VI.

NALA, chosen by Bhima's daughter—the bright guardians of the world,
As they parted thence, with Kali—Dwapara approaching saw.
Kali as he saw, did Indra—did the giant-killer say,
"Here, with Dwapara attended—whither, Kali, dost thou go?"
Kali spake, "the Swayembara—we of Damayanti seek;
"Her I go to make my consort—into her mine heart hath passed."
"Closed and ended is that bridal,"—Indra answered with a smile,
"Nala she hath chosen for husband—in the presence of us all."
Thus addressed by Indra, Kali—in the transport of his wrath,
All the heavenly gods saluting,—thus his malediction spake,
"Since before the Immortals' presence—she a mortal spouse did choose,
"Of her impious crime most justly—heavy be the penal doom."
Kali hardly thus had spoken—than the heaven-born gods replied:
"With our full and liberal sanction—Damayanti chose her lord.
"Who to Nala, with all virtue—rich endowed, would not incline?
"He that rightly knows each duty—he who ever rightly acts,
"He who reads the whole four Vedas—the Puranas too the fifth,
"In his palace with pure offerings—ever are the gods adored,
"Gentle to all living creatures—true in word and strict in vow;
"Good and constant he, and generous—holy, temperate, patient, pure;
"His are all these virtues ever—equal to the earth-guarding gods.
"Thus endowed, the noble Nala—he, O Kali, that would curse,
"On himself recoil his curses—only fatal to himself.
"Nala, gifted with such virtues—he, O Kali, who would curse—

"Be he plunged in hell's dark torments—in the deep and vasty lake."
Thus the gods to Kali speaking—to their native heavens arose.
Soon as they had parted, Kali—thus to Dwapara began:
"I my wrath can curb no longer—I henceforth in Nala dwell;
"From his kingdom will I cast him—from his bliss with his sweet bride.
"Thou within the dice embodied—Dwapara my cause assist."

BOOK VII.

Bound by that malignant treaty—Kali with his dark ally,
Haunted they the stately palace—where Nishadha's monarch ruled;
Watching still the fatal instant—in Nishadha long they dwelt.
Twelve long years had passed ere Kali—saw that fatal instant come.
Nala after act uncleanly—the ablution half performed,
Prayed at eve, with feet unwashen—Kali seized the fatal hour.
Into Nala straight he entered—and possessed his inmost soul.
Pushkara in haste he summoned—come with Nala play at dice,
Ever in the gainful hazard—by my subtle aid thou'lt win,
Even the kingdom of Nishadha—even from Nala all his realm.
Pushkara by Kali summoned—to his brother Nala came,
In the dice of dice embodied—Dwapara stood silent by.
Pushkara the hero-slayer—to king Nala standing near:
"Play we with the dice, my brother,"—thus again, again he said.
Long the lofty-minded raja—that bold challenge might not brook,
In Vidarbha's princess' presence—deemed he now the time for play.
For his wealth, his golden treasures—for his chariots, for his robes,
Then possessed by Kali, Nala—in the game was worsted still.
He with love of gaming maddened,—of his faithful friends not one
Might arrest the desperate frenzy—of the conqueror of his foes.
Came the citizens assembling—with the counsellors of state,
To behold the king approached they—to restrain his dread disease.
Then the charioteer advancing—thus to Damayanti spake:
"All the city, noble princess—stands assembled at the gate,
"Say thou to Nishadha's monarch—'All his subjects here are met;

" 'Ill they brook this dire misfortune—in their justice-loving king'."
Then, her voice half choked with anguish—spake the sorrow-stricken queen,
Spirit-broken, Bhima's daughter—to Nishadha's sovereign spake,
" Raja, lo! the assembled city—at the gate their king to see:
" With the counsellors of wisdom—by their loyal duty led.
" Deign thou, monarch, to admit them,"—thus again, again she said.
To the queen with beauteous eyelids—uttering thus her sad lament,
Still possessed by wicked Kali—answered not the king a word.
Then those counsellors of wisdom—and those loyal citizens,
" 'Tis not he," exclaimed in sorrow,—and in shame and grief went home.
Thus of Pushkara and Nala—still went on that fatal play;
Many a weary month it lasted—and still lost the king of men.

BOOK VIII.

DAMAYANTI then beholding—Punyasloka, king of men,
Undistracted, him distracted—with the maddening love of play.
In her dread and in her sorrow—thus did Bhima's daughter speak;
Pondering on the weighty business—that concerned the king of men.
Trembling at his guilty frenzy—yet to please him still intent.
Nala, 'reft of all his treasures—when the noble woman saw,
Thus addressed she Vrihatsena,—her old faithful slave and nurse,
Friendly in all business dextrous—most devoted, wise in speech:
" Vrihatsena, go, the council—as at Nala's call convene,
" Say what he hath lost of treasure—and what treasure yet remains."
Then did all that reverend council—Nala's summons as they heard,
" Our own fate is now in peril"—speaking thus, approach the king.
And a second time his subjects—all assembling, crowded near,
And the queen announced their presence;—of her words he took no heed.
All her words thus disregarded—when king Bhima's daughter found,
To the palace, Damayanti—to conceal her shame returned.
When the dice she heard for ever—adverse to the king of men,
And of all bereft, her Nala—to the nurse again she spake:
" Go again, my Vrihatsena,—in the name of Nala, go,
" To the charioteer, Varshneya,—great the deed must now be done."
Vrihatsena on the instant—Damayanti's words she heard,
Caused the charioteer be summoned—by her messengers of trust.
Bhima's daughter to Varshneya—winning with her gentle voice,
Spake, the time, the place well choosing—for the deed, nor spake in vain:
" Well thou know'st the full reliance—that in thee the king hath placed,

"In his fatal hour of peril—wilt not thou stand forth to aid?
"As by Pushkara is worsted—ever more and more the king,
"More and more the fatal frenzy—maddens in his heart for play.
"As to Pushkara obedient—ever fall the lucky dice,
"Thus those dice to royal Nala—still with adverse fortune fall.
"Nor the voice of friend or kindred—as beseems him, will he hear;
"Even to me he will not listen—in the madness of his heart.
"Of the lofty-minded Nala—well I know 'tis not the sin,
"That my words this senseless monarch—in his frenzy will not hear.
"Charioteer, to thee my refuge—come I, do thou my behest;
"I am not o'er calm in spirit—haply he may perish thus.
"Yoke the much-loved steeds of Nala—fleet of foot, as thought, are they,
"In the chariot place our children—to Cundina's city go.
"Leave the children with my kindred—and the chariot and the steeds;
"Then or dwell there at thy pleasure—or depart where'er thou wilt."
When the speech of Damayanti—heard king Nala's charioteer,
He, the chief of Nala's council—thus in full divan addressed,
Weighed within their solemn conclave—and their full assent obtained,
With the children in the chariot—to Vidarbha straight he drove.
There he rendered up the horses—with the chariot there he left.
That young maiden Indrasena—Indrasen, that noble boy.
To king Bhima paid his homage—sad, for Nala's fall distressed,
Thence departing, to Ayodhya—took the charioteer his way.
In his grief to Rituparna—that illustrious king, he came,
As his charioteer, the service—entered of the lord of earth.

BOOK IX.

SCARCE Varshneya had departed—still the king of men played on,
Till to Pushkara his kingdom—all that he possessed, was lost.
Nala then, despoiled of kingdom—smiling Pushkara bespake:
"Throw we yet another hazard—Nala, where is now thy stake?
"There remains but Damayanti—all thou hast beside, is mine.
"Throw we now for Damayanti—come, once more the hazard try."
Thus as Pushkara addressed him—Punyasloka's inmost heart
By his grief was rent asunder—not a single word he spake.
And on Pushkara, king Nala—in his silent anguish gazed.
All his ornaments of splendour—from his person stripped he off,
With a single vest, scarce covered,—'mid the sorrow of his friends,
Slowly wandered forth the monarch—fallen from such an height of bliss.
Damayanti with one garment—slowly followed him behind.
Three long nights Nishadha's monarch—there without the gates had dwelt.
Proclamation through the city—then did Pushkara bid make,
"Whosoe'er befriendeth Nala—shall to instant death be doomed."
Thus, as Pushkara gave order—in the terror of his power,
Might the citizens no longer—hospitably serve the king.
Near the walls, of kind reception—worthiest, but by none received;
Three nights longer staid the monarch—water was his only drink,
He in unfastidious hunger—plucked the fruits, the roots of earth.
Then went forth again the outcast:—Damayanti followed slow.
In the agony of famine—Nala, after many days,
Saw some birds around him settling—with their golden tinctured wings.
Then the monarch of Nishadha—thought within his secret heart,

These to-day my welcome banquet—and my treasure these will be.
Over them his single garment—spreading light he wrapped them round:
Up that single garment bearing—to the air they sprang away;
And the birds above him hovering—thus in human accents spake,
Naked as they saw him standing—on the earth, and sad, and lone:—
" Lo, we are the dice, to spoil thee—thus descended, foolish king!
" While thou hadst a single garment—all our joy was incomplete."
When the dice he saw departing—and himself without his robe,
Mournfully did Punyasloka—thus to Damayanti speak:
" They, O blameless, by whose anger—from my kingdom I am driven,
" Life-sustaining food unable—in my misery to find—
" They, through whom Nishadha's people—may not house their outcast king—
" They, the forms of birds assuming—my one robe have borne away.
" In the dark extreme of misery—sad and frantic as I am,
" Hear me, princess, hear and profit—by thy husband's best advice.
" Hence are many roads diverging—to the region of the south,
" Passing by Avanti's city—and the height of Rishavàn;
" Vindhya here, the mighty mountain—and Payoshni's seaward stream;
" And the lone retreats of hermits—on the fruits of earth that live;
" This will lead thee to Vidarbha—this to Cosala away,
" Far beyond the region stretches—southward to the southward clime."
In these words to Damayanti—did the royal Nala speak,
More than once to Bhima's daughter—anxious pointing out the way.
She, with voice half choked with sorrow—with her weight of woe oppressed,
These sad words did Damayanti—to Nishadha's monarch speak:—
" My afflicted heart is breaking—and my sinking members fail,
" When, O king, thy desperate counsel—once I think of, once again.
" Robbed of kingdom, robbed of riches—naked, thirst and hunger worn;

E

" How shall I depart and leave thee—in the wood by man untrod.
" When thou sad and famine-stricken—thinkest of thy former bliss,
" In the wild wood, oh, my husband,—I thy weariness will soothe.
" Like a wife, in every sorrow—this the wise physicians own,
" Healing herb is none or balsam—Nala, 'tis the truth I speak."

NALA *spake.*

Slender-waisted Damayanti—true, indeed, is all thou'st said;
Like a wife no friendly medicine—to afflicted man is given.
Fear not that I thee abandon—Wherefore, timid, dread'st thou this?
Oh, myself might I abandon—and not thee, thou unreproached.

DAMAYANTI *spake.*

If indeed, oh mighty monarch—thou wilt ne'er abandon me,
Wherefore then towards Vidarbha—dost thou point me out the way.
Well, I know thee, noble Nala—to desert me far too true,
Only with a soul distracted—would'st thou leave me, lord of earth.
Yet, again, the way thou pointest—yet, again, thou best of men,
Thus my sorrow still enhancing—oh, thou like the immortal gods;
If this be thy better counsel—'to her kindred let her go,'
Be it so, and both together—to Vidarbha set we forth.
Thee Vidarbha's king will honour—honour'd in his turn by thee;
Held in high respect and happy—in our mansion thou shalt dwell.

BOOK X.

Nala *spake.*

"Mighty is thy father's kingdom—once was mine as mighty too;
Never will I there seek refuge—in my base extremity.
There I once appeared in glory—to the exalting of thy pride;
Shall I now appear in misery—to the increasing of thy shame?"
Nala thus to Damayanti—spake again, and yet again,
Comforting the noble lady—scant in half a garment clad.
Both together by one garment—covered, roamed they here and there;
Wearied out by thirst and famine—to a cabin drew they near.
When they reached that lowly cabin—then did great Nishadha's king
With the princess of Vidarbha—on the hard earth seat them down;
Naked, with no mat to rest on—wet with mire and stained with dust.
Weary then with Damayanti—on the earth he fell asleep.
Sank the lovely Damayanti—by his side with sleep opprest,
She thus plunged in sudden misery—she the tender, the devout.
But while on the cold earth slumbered—Damayanti, all distraught
Nala in his mind by sorrow—might no longer calmly sleep;
For the losing of his kingdom—the desertion of his friends,
And his weary forest wanderings—painful on his thought arose;
"If I do it, what may follow?—what if I refuse to do?
Were my instant death the better—or to abandon her I love.
But to me too deep devoted—suffers she distress and shame;
Reft of me she home may wander—to her royal father's house;
Faithful wandering ever with me—certain sorrow will she bear,

E 2

But if separated from me—chance of solace may be hers."
Long within his heart he pondered—and again, again weighed o'er.
Best he thought it Damayanti—to desert, that wretched king.
From her virtue none dare harm her—in the lonely forest way,
Her the fortunate, the noble—my devoted wedded wife.
Thus his mind on Damayanti—dwelt in its perverted thought,
Wrought by Kali's evil influence—to desert his lovely wife.
Of himself without a garment—and of her with only one
As he thought, approached he near her—to divide that single robe.
"How shall I divide the garment—by my loved one unperceived?"
Pondering this within his spirit—round the cabin Nala went;
In that narrow cabin's circuit—Nala wandered here and there,
Till he found without a scabbard—shining, a well-tempered sword.
Then when half that only garment—he had severed, and put on,
In her sleep Vidarbha's princess—with bewildered mind he fled.
Yet, his cruel heart relenting—to the cabin turns he back;
On the slumbering Damayanti—gazing, sadly wept the king;
Thou, that sun nor wind hath ever—roughly visited, my love!
On the hard earth in a cabin—sleepest with thy guardian gone.
Thus attired in half a garment—she that aye so sweetly smiled,
Like to one distracted, beauteous—how at length will she awake?
How will't fare with Bhima's daughter—lone, abandoned by her lord,
Wandering in the savage forest—where wild beasts and serpents dwell.
May the suns and winds of heaven—may the genii of the woods,
Noblest, may they all protect thee—thine own virtue thy best guard."
To his wife of peerless beauty—on the earth, 'twas thus he spoke.
Then of sense bereft by Kali—Nala hastily set forth;
And departing, still departing—he returned again, again;

Dragged away by that bad demon—ever by his love drawn back.
Nala, thus his heart divided—into two conflicting parts,
Like a swing goes backward, forward—from the cabin, to and fro.
Torn away at length by Kali—flies afar the frantic king,
Leaving there his wife in slumber—making miserable moans.
Reft of sense, possessed by Kali—thinking still on her he left,
Passed he in the lonely forest—leaving his deserted wife.

BOOK XI.

SCARCELY had king Nala parted—Damayanti now refreshed,
Wakened up, the slender-waisted—timorous in the desert wood.
When she did not see her husband—overpowered with grief and pain,
Loud she shriek'd in her first anguish—"Where art thou, Nishadha's king?
"Mighty king! my soul-protector—O, my lord! desert'st thou me.
"Oh, I'm lost! undone for ever—helpless in the wild wood left;
"Faithful once to every duty—wert thou not, and true in word.
"Art thou faithful to thy promise—to desert me thus in sleep.
"Could'st thou then depart, forsaking—thy devoted, constant wife;
"Her in sooth that never wronged thee—wronged indeed, but not by her.
"Keep'st thou thus thy solemn promise—oh, unfaithful lord of men,
"There, when all the gods were present—plighted to thy wedded wife?
"Death is but decreed to mortals—at its own appointed time,
"Hence one moment, thus deserted—one brief moment do I live.—
"But thou'st had thy sport—enough then—now desist, O king of men,
"Mock not thou a trembling woman—show thee to me, O my lord!
"Yes, I see thee, there I see thee—hidden as thou think'st from sight,
"In the rushes why conceal thee?—answer me, why speak'st thou not.
"Wherefore now ungentle stay'st thou—like to one forsworn, aloof?
"Wherefore wilt thou not approach me—to console me in my woe?
"For myself I will not sorrow—nor for aught to me befalls.
"Thou art all alone, my husband,—I will only mourn for thee.
"How will't fare with thee, my Nala—thirsting, famished, faint with toil.
"Nor beholding me await thee—underneath the trees at eve."
Then, in all her depth of anguish—with her trouble as on fire,

Hither, thither, went she weeping—all around she went and wailed.
Now springs up the desolate princess—now falls down in prostrate grief;
Now she pines in silent sorrow—now she shrieks and wails aloud.
So consumed with inward misery—ever sighing more and more,
Spake at length king Bhima's daughter—spake the still devoted wife:
" He, by whose dire imprecation—Nala this dread suffering bears,
" May he far surpass in suffering—all that Nala suffers now.
" May the evil one, to evil—who the blameless Nala drives,
" Smitten by a curse as fatal—live a dark unblessed life."
Thus her absent lord lamenting—that high-minded raja's queen,
Every-where her lord went seeking—in the satyr-haunted wood.
Like a maniac, Bhima's daughter—wandered wailing here and there;
And "alas! alas! my husband"—every-where her cry was heard.
Her beyond all measure wailing—like the osprey screaming shrill,
Miserably still deploring—still renewing her lament.
Suddenly king Bhima's daughter—as she wandered near his lair,
Siezed a huge gigantic serpent—in his raging famine fierce.
In the grasp of that fierce serpent—round about with terror girt,
Not herself she pities only—pities she Nishadha's king.
" O my guardian, thus unguarded—in this savage forest seized,
" Seized by this terrific serpent—wherefore art not thou at hand?
" How will't be, when thou rememberest—once again thy faithful wife,
" From this dreadful curse delivered—mind, and sense, and wealth returned?
" When thou'rt weary, when thou'rt hungry—when thou'rt fainting with fatigue,
" Who will soothe, O blameless Nala—all thy weariness, thy woe."

Then a huntsman as he wandered—in the forest jungle thick,
As he heard her thus bewailing—in his utmost haste drew near.
In the grasp when he beheld her—of that long-eyed serpent fell,

Instant did the nimble huntsman—rapidly as he came on,
Pierce that unresisting serpent—with a sharp and mortal shaft:
In her sight he slew that serpent—skill'd in slaughter of the chase.
Her released he from her peril—washed he then with water pure,
And with sylvan food refreshed her—and with soothing words address'd:
"Who art thou that roam'st the forest—with the eyes of the gazelle;
"How to this extreme of misery—noble lady, hast thou fallen?"
Damayanti, by the huntsman—thus in soothing tone addressed,
All the story of her misery—told him, as it all befell;
Her, scant-clothed in half a garment—with soft swelling limbs and breast,
Form of youthful faultless beauty—and her fair and moonlike face,
And her eyes with brows dark arching—and her softly-melting speech,
Saw long time that wild beast hunter—kindled all his heart with love.
Then with winning voice that huntsman—bland beginning his discourse,
Fain with amorous speech would soothe her—she his dark intent perceived.
Damayanti, chaste and faithful,—soon as she his meaning knew,
In the transport of her anger—her indignant soul took fire.
In his wicked thought the dastard—her yet powerless to subdue,
On the unsubdued stood gazing—as like some bright flame she shone.
Damayanti, in her sorrow—of her realm, her lord bereft,
On the instant she found language—uttered loud her curse of wrath,—
"As my pure and constant spirit—swerves not from Nishadha's lord,
"Instant so may this base hunter—lifeless fall upon the earth."
Scarce that single word was uttered—suddenly that hunter bold
Down upon the earth fell lifeless—like a lightning blasted tree.

BOOK XII.

Slain that savage wild-beast hunter—onward went the lotus-eyed,
Through the dread, and desert forest—ringing with the cricket's song;
Full of lions, pards, and tigers—stags, and buffalos, and bears,
Where all kinds of birds were flocking—and wild men and robbers dwelt.
Trees of every form and stature—every foliage, every name;
Pregnant with rich mines of metal—many a mountain it enclosed,
Many a shady resonant arbour—many a deep and wondrous glen;
Many a lake, and pool, and river—birds and beasts of every shape.
She, in forms terrific round her—serpents, elves, and giants saw:
Pools, and tanks of lucid water—and the shaggy tops of hills,
Flowing streams and headlong torrents—saw, and wondered at the sight.
And the princess of Vidarbha—gazed where in their countless herds,
Buffalos and bears were feeding—boars, and serpents of the wood.
Safe in virtue, bright in beauty—glorious and of high resolve,
Now alone, Vidarbha's daughter—wandering, her lost Nala sought.
Yet no fear king Bhima's daughter—for herself might deign to feel,
Travelling the dreary forest—only for her lord distressed;
Him she mourned, that noble princess—him in bitterest anguish wailed,
Every limb with sorrow trembling—stood she on a beetling rock;
" Monarch, with broad chest capacious—monarch with the sinewy arm,
Me in this dread forest leaving—whither hast thou fled away?
Thou the holy Aswamedha—thou each sacrificial rite,
Hast performed, to me, me only—in thy holy faith thou'st failed.
That which thou, O best of husbands—in mine hearing hast declared,

F

Thy most solemn vow remember—call to mind thy plighted faith.
Of the swift-winged swans the language—uttered, monarch, by thy side,
That thyself, before my presence—didst renew, bethink thee well.
Thou the Vedas, thou the Angas—with the Upangas oft hast read,
Of each heaven-descended volume—one and simple is the truth.
Therefore, of thy foes the slayer!—reverence thou the sacred truth
Of thy solemn plighted promise—in my presence sworn so oft.
Am not I the loved so dearly—purely, sinlessly beloved;
In this dark and awful forest—wherefore dost thou not reply?
Here with monstrous jaws wide yawning—with his fierce and horrid form,
Gapes the forest king to slay me—and thou art not here to save.
None but I, thou'st said, for ever—none but I to thee am dear!
Make this oft-repeated language—make this oft-sworn promise true.
To thy queen bereft of reason—to thy weeping wife beloved,
Why repliest thou not—her only thou desir'st—she only thee.
Meagre, miserable, pallid—tainted with the dust and mire,
Scantly clad in half a garment—lone, with no protector near;
Like a large-eyed hind that wanders—separate from the wonted herd,
Thou regard'st me not, thus weeping—oh thou tamer of thy foes.
Mighty king, a lonely wanderer—in this vast and trackless wood,
Damayanti, I address thee—wherefore answerest not my voice?
Nobly born, and nobly minded—beautiful in every limb,
Do I not e'en now behold thee—in this mountain, first of men,
In this lion-haunted forest—in this tiger-howling wood,
Lying down or seated, standing—or in majesty and might
Moving, do I not behold thee—the enhancer of my woe?
Who shall I address, afflicted—wasted by my grief away;
'Hast thou haply seen my Nala—in the solitary wood?'

Who this day will show the monarch—wandering in the forest depth,
Beautiful and royal-minded—conqueror of an host of foes!
'Him thou seek'st with eyes of lotus—Nala, sovereign of men—
Lo, he's here!' whose voice of music—may I hear thus sweetly speak?
Lo, with fourfold tusks before me—and with wide and gaping jaws,
Stands the forest king, the tiger—I approach him without fear.
"Of the beasts art thou the monarch—all this forest thy domain,
For the daughter of Vidarbha—Damayanti, know thou me,
Consort of Nishadha's sovereign—Nala, slayer of his foes—
Seeking here my exile husband—lonely, wretched, sorrow-driven,
Thou, O king of beasts, console me—if my Nala thou hast seen;
Or, O lord of all the forest—Nala if thou canst not show,
Best of savage beasts, devour me—from my misery set me free.
Hearing thus my lamentation—now does that fell king of beasts
Go towards the crystal river—flowing downward to the sea.'—
To this mountain then the holy—crowned with many a lofty peak,
In its soul-exalting splendour—rising, many-hued, to heaven;
Full within of precious metal—rich with many a glowing gem,
Rising o'er the spreading forest—like a banner broad and high,
Ranged by elephants and lions—tigers, bears, and boars, and stags;
And of many birds the voices—sweetly sound o'er all its cliffs;
All the trees of richest foliage—all the trees of stateliest height,
All the flowers and golden fruitage—on its crested summits wave,
Down its peaks in many a streamlet—dip the water-birds their wings:
This, the monarch of all mountains—ask I of the king of men;
'O, all-honoured Prince of Mountains, with thy heaven-ward soaring peaks,
Refuge of the lost, most noble—thee, O Mountain, I salute;
I salute thee, lowly bowing—I, the daughter of a king;

Of a king the royal consort—of a king's son I the bride.
Of Vidarbha the great sovereign—mighty hero is my sire,
Named the lord of earth, king Bhima—of each caste the guardian he;
Of the holy Aswamedha—of the regal sacrifice,
He the offerer, best of monarchs—known by his commanding eye,
Pious, and of life unblemished—true in word, of generous speech,
Affable, courageous, prosperous—skilled in every duty, pure,
Of Vidarbha the protector—conqueror of a host of foes;
Know me of that king the daughter—lowly thus approaching thee.
In Nishadha, mighty Mountain! dwelt the father of my lord,
High the name he won, the illustrious—Virasena was he called.
Of this king the son, the hero—prosperous and truly brave,
He who rules his father's kingdom—by hereditary right,
Slayer of his foes, dark Nala—Punyasloka is he called;
Holy, Veda read, and eloquent—soma quaffing, fire adoring,
Sacrificer, liberal giver—warrior, in all points a king,—
Of this monarch, best of mountains—know, the wife before thee stands,
Fallen from bliss, bereft of husband—unprotected, sorrow-doomed,
Seeking every where her husband—him the best of noblest men.
Best of mountains, heaven-upsoaring—with thy hundred stately peaks,
Hast thou seen the kingly Nala—in this dark and awful wood:
Like the elephant in courage—wise, impetuous, with long arms,
Valiant, and of truth unquestioned—my heroic, glorious lord;
Hast thou seen Nishadha's sovereign—mighty Nala hast thou seen?
Why repliest thou not, oh Mountain—sorrowing, lonely, and distressed,
With thy voice why not console me—as thine own afflicted child?

Hero, mighty, strong in duty—true of promise, lord of earth,
If thou art within the forest—show thee in thy proper form.

When so eloquently deep-toned—like the sound of some dark cloud,
Shall I hear thy voice, oh Nala!—sweet as the amrita draught,
Saying, 'daughter of Vidarbha!'—with distinct, with blessed sound,
Musical as holy Veda—rich, and soothing all my pain;
Thus console me, trembling, fainting—thou, oh virtue-loving king!"
To the holiest of mountains—spake the daughter of the king.
Damayanti then set forward—toward the region of the north.
Three days long, three nights she wandered—then that noble woman saw,
The unrivalled wood of hermits—like to a celestial grove.
To the ancient famous hermits—equal was that sacred crew;
Self-denying, strict in diet—temperate, and undefiled;
Water-drinking, air inhaling—and the leaves their simple food;
Mortified, for ever blessed—seeking the right way to heaven;
Bark for vests and skins for raiment—wore those hermits, sense-subdued.
She beheld the pleasant circle—of those hermits' lonely cells;
Round them flocks of beasts were grazing—wantoned there the monkey tribes.
When she saw those holy dwellings—all her courage was revived.
Lovely browed, and lovely tressed—lovely bosom'd, lovely lipp'd,
In her brightness, in her glory—with her large dark beauteous eyes,
Entered she those hermit dwellings—wife of Virasena's son;
Pearl of women, ever blessed—Damayanti the devout,
She those holy men saluting—stood with modest form half bent.
"Hail, and welcome!" thus those hermits—instant with one voice exclaimed.
And those sacred men no sooner—had the fitting homage paid,
"Take thy seat," they said, "oh lady—and command what we must do."
Thus replied the slender waisted—"Blessed are ye, holy men.
"In your sacred fires, your worship—blameless, with your beasts and birds.
"Doth the grace of heaven attend you—in your duties, in your deeds?"

Answered they, " The grace of heaven—ever blesses all our deeds.
" But say thou, of form so beauteous—who thou art, and what thou would'st?
" As thy noble form we gaze on—on thy brightness as we gaze,
" In amaze we stand and wonder—cheer thee up, and mourn no more.
" Of the wood art thou the goddess—or the mountain goddess thou;
" Or the goddess of the river?—Blessed Spirit, speak the truth."
" Nor the sylvan goddess am I,"—to the Wise she thus replied;
" Neither of the mountain, Brahmins—nor the river nymph am I.
" Know me but a mortal being—O, ye rich in holiness!
" All my tale at length, I'll tell ye—if meet audience ye will give.
" In Vidarbha, mighty guardian—Bhima, dwells the lord of earth;
" Of that noble king the daughter—twice-born Sages, know ye me.
" And the monarch of Nishadha—Nala named, the great in fame;
" Brave in battle, conqueror, prudent—is my lord, the peasants' king;
" To the gods devout in worship—friendly to the Brahmin race,
" Of Nishadha's race the guardian—great in glory, great in might,
" True in word, and skilled in duty—and the slayer of his foes.
" Pious, heaven-devoted, prosperous—conqueror of hostile towns;
" Nala named, the best of sovereigns—splendid as the king of gods.
" Know that large-eyed chief, my husband—like the full-orbed moon his face,
" Giver he of costly offerings—deep in th' holy volumes read;
" Slayer of his foes in battle—glorious as the sun and moon.
" He to some most evil minded—unrespected, wicked men,
" After many a challenge, studious—he of virtue and of truth,
" To these skilful gamesters, fraudful—lost his kingdom and his wealth.
" Know ye me the hapless consort—of that noble king of kings,
" Damayanti, so they name me—yearning for my husband's sight.
" I through forests, over mountains—stagnant marsh and river broad,

"Lake with wide pellucid surface—through the long and trackless wood,
"Ever seeking for my husband—Nala, skilful in the fight.
"Mighty in the use of weapons—wander desolate and sad.
"Tell me, to this pleasant sojourn—sacred to these holy men,
"Hath he come, the royal Nala?—hath Nishadha's monarch come?
"For whose sake through ways all trackless—terrible, have I set forth,
"In this drear, appalling forest—where the lynx and tiger range,
"If I see not noble Nala—ere few days, few nights are o'er,
"I to happiness will join me—from this mortal frame set free.
"Reft of him, my princely husband—what have I to do with life—
"How endure existence longer—for my husband thus distressed."
To the lady thus complaining—lonely in the savage wood,
Answered thus those holy hermits—spake the gifted seers the truth:—
"There will be a time hereafter—beautiful, the time will come,
"Through devotion now we see him—and thou too wilt see him soon;
"That good monarch of Nishadha—Nala, slayer of his foes;
"That dispenser of strict justice—Bhima's daughter! free from grief,
"From all sin released, thou'lt see him—glittering in his royal gems,
"Governing that noble city—o'er his enemies supreme.
"To his foemen causing terror—to his friends allaying grief,
"Thou, oh noble, shalt thy husband—see, that king of noble race."
To the much-loved wife of Nala—to the princess speaking thus,
Vanished then those holy hermits—with their sacred fires, their cells.
As she gazed upon the wonder—wrapt in mute amaze she stood;
Damayanti, fair-limbed princess—wife of Virasena's son;
"Have I only seen a vision—what hath been this wondrous chance?
Where are all those holy hermits—where the circle of their cells?
Where that pure and pleasant river—haunted by the dipping birds?

Where those trees with grateful umbrage—with their pendant fruits and flowers?"
Long within her heart she pondered—Damayanti with sweet smile,
For her lord, to grief abandoned—miserable, pale of hue;
To another region passed she—there with voice by weeping choked,
Mourns she, till with eyes o'erflowing—an Asoca tree she saw.
Best of trees, the Asoca blooming—in the forest she approached,
Gemmed all o'er with glowing fruitage—vocal with the songs of birds.
"Ah, behold amid the forest—flourishes this happy tree,
With its leafy garlands radiant—as the joyous mountain king.
O thou tree with pleasant aspect—from my sorrow set me free.
Vitasoca, hast thou seen him—hast the fearless raja seen,
Nala, of his foes the slayer—Damayanti's lord beloved?
Hast thou seen Nishadha's monarch—hast thou seen mine only love,
Clad in half a single garment—with his soft and delicate skin;
Hast thou seen th' afflicted hero—wandering in the forest lone.
That I may depart ungrieving—fair Asoca, answer me.
Truly be thou named Asoca—as the extinguisher of grief."
Thus in her o'erpowering anguish—moved she round the Asoca tree.
Then she went her way in sadness—to another region dread.
Many a tree she stood and gazed on—many a river passed she o'er;
Passed she many a pleasant mountain—many a wild deer, many a bird;
Many a hill and many a cavern—many a bright and wondrous stream,
Saw king Bhima's wandering daughter—as she sought her husband lost.
Long she roamed her weary journey—Damayanti with sweet smile,
Lo, a caravan of merchants—elephants, and steeds, and cars,
And beyond, a pleasant river—with its waters cool and clear.
'Twas a quiet stream, and waveless—girt about with spreading canes;

There the cuckoo, there the osprey—there the red-geese clamouring stood;
Swarmed the turtles, fish and serpents—there rose many a stately isle.
When she saw that numerous concourse—Nala's once all-glorious wife,
Entered she, the slender-waisted—in the midst of all the host;
Maniac-like in form and feature—and in half a garment clad,
Thin and pallid, travel-tainted—matted all her locks with dust.
As they all beheld her standing—some in terror fled away;
Some stood still in speechless wonder—others raised their voice and cried;
Mocked her some with cruel tauntings—others spake reproachful words;
Others looked on her with pity—and enquired her state, her name.
"Who art thou? whose daughter, Lady—in the forest seek'st thou aught?
"At thy sight we stand confounded—art thou of our mortal race?
"Of this wood art thou the goddess?—of this mountain? of that plain?
"Who art thou, O noble Lady—thee, our refuge, we adore.
"Art thou sylvan nymph or genius—or celestial nymph divine?
"Every-way regard our welfare—and protect us, undespised:
"So our caravan in safety—may pursue its onward way,
"So ordain it, O illustrious!—that good fortune wait on all."
Thus addressed by that assemblage—Damayanti, kingly-born,
Answered thus with gentle language—grieving for her husband lost.
Of that caravan the leader—and the whole assembled host,
Youths and boys, and grey-haired elders—and the guides, thus answered she:
"Know me, like yourselves, a mortal—daughter of a king of men,
"Of another king the consort—seeking for my royal lord;
"Know, Vidarbha's king, my father—and Nishadha's king, my lord,
"Nala, is his name, the glorious—him, th' unconquered do I seek;
"Know ye aught of that good monarch—tell me, quick, of my beloved,
"Of the tiger hero, Nala—slayer of a host of foes."

G

Of the caravan the captain—thus the lovely-limbed addressed,
Suchi was his name, the merchant—" Hear, illustrious queen, my speech;
" Of this caravan the captain—I, O Lady with sweet smile,
" Him that bears the name of Nala—nowhere have these eyes beheld.
" Elephants, and pards, and tigers—lynxes, buffaloes, and bears,
" See I in this trackless forest—uninhabited by men;
" Save thyself, of human feature—nought, or human form, I've seen.
" So may he, the king of Yakshas—Manibhadra, guard us well."
To the merchants then she answered—to the leader of the host,
" Tell me whither do ye travel?—whither bound your caravan?"

The CAPTAIN *of the caravan spake.*

" To the realm of Chedi's sovereign—truth-discerning Subahu,
" Soon this caravan will enter—travelling in search of gain."

BOOK XIII.

This, the lovely princess hearing—from the captain of the band,
With the caravan set forward—seeking still her royal lord.
Long their journey through the forest—through the dark and awful glens;
Then a lake of loveliest beauty—fragrant with the lotus flowers,
Saw those merchants, wide and pleasant—with fresh grass and shady trees;
Flowers and fruits bedecked its borders—where the birds melodious sang:
In its clear delicious waters—soul-enchanting, icy cool,
With their horses all o'erwearied—thought they then to plunge and bathe;
At the signal of the captain—entered all that pleasant grove.
At the close of day arriving—there encamped they for the night.
When the midnight came, all noiseless—came in silence deep and still,
Weary slept the band of merchants—lo, a herd of elephants,
Oozing moisture from their temples—came to drink the troubled stream.
When that caravan they gazed on—with their slumbering beasts at rest,
The tame elephants they scented—those wild forest elephants;
Forward rush they fleet and furious—mad to slay, and wild with heat;
Irresistible the onset—of the rushing ponderous beasts,
As the peaks from some high mountain—down the valley thundering roll;
Strewn was all the way before them—with the boughs, the trunks of trees;
On they crash'd to where the travellers—slumbered by the lotus lake.
Trampled down without a struggle—helpless on the earth they lay,
"Woe, oh, woe!" shrieked out the merchants—wildly some began to fly,
In the forest thickets' plunging;—some stood gasping, blind with sleep;
And the elephants down beat them—with their tusks, their trunks, their feet.

Many saw their camels dying—mingled with the men on foot,
And in frantic tumult rushing—wildly struck each other down;
Many miserably shrieking—cast them down upon the earth,
Many climbed the trees in terror—on the rough ground stumbled some.
Thus in various wise and fatal—by the elephants assailed,
Lay that caravan so wealthy—scattered all abroad or slain.
Such, so fearful was the tumult—the three worlds seemed all appalled,
" 'Tis a fire amid th' encampment—save ye, fly ye, for your lives.
" Lo, your precious pearls ye trample—take them up, why fly so fast?
" Save them, 'tis a common venture—fear ye not that I deceive."
Thus t' each other shrieked the merchants—as in fear they scattered round.
" Yet again I call upon you—cowards! think ye what ye do."
All around this frantic carnage—raging through the prostrate host,
Damayanti, soon awakened—with her heart all full of dread;
There she saw a hideous slaughter—the whole world might well appal.
To such sights all unfamiliar—gazed the queen with lotus eyes,
Pressing in her breath with terror—slowly rose she on her feet.
And the few that scaped the carnage—few that scaped without a wound,
All at once exclaimed together—" Of whose deeds is this the doom?"
" Hath not mighty Manibhadra—adoration meet received.
" And Vaisravana the holy—of the Yakshas lord and king,
" Have not all that might impede us—ere we journied, been addressed?
" Was it doomed, that all good omens—by this chance should be belied?
" Were no planets haply adverse?—how hath fate, like this, befall'n!"
Others answered in their misery—reft of kindred and of wealth,
" Who is that ill-omened woman—that with maniac-staring eyes,
" Joined our host, mis-shaped in aspect—and with scarcely human form?
" Surely all this wicked witchcraft—by her evil power is wrought;

"Witch or sorceress she, or dæmon—fatal cause of all our fears,
"Hers is all the guilt, the misery—who such damning proof may doubt?
"Could we but behold that false one—murtheress, bane of all our host,
"With the clods, the dust, the bamboos—with our staves, or with our hands,
"We would slay her on the instant—of our caravan the fate."
But no sooner Damayanti—their appalling words had heard,
In her shame and in her terror—to the forest shade she fled.
And that guilt imputed dreading—thus her fate began to wail:
"Woe is me, still o'er me hovers—the terrific wrath of fate;
"No good fortune e'er attends me—of what guilt is this the doom?
"Not a sin can I remember—not the least to living man.
"Or in deed, or thought, or language—of what guilt is this the doom?
"In some former life committed—expiate I now the sin.
"To this infinite misfortune—hence by penal justice doomed?
"Lost my husband, lost my kingdom—from my kindred separate;
"Separate from noble Nala—from my children far away,
"Widowed of my rightful guardian—in the serpent-haunted wood."
Of that caravan at morning—then the sad surviving few,
Setting forth from that dread region—o'er that hideous carnage grieve;
Each a brother mourns, or father—or a son, or dearest friend,
Still Vidarbha's princess uttered—"What the sin that I have done?
"Scarcely in this desert forest—had I met this host of men,
"By the elephants they perish—this is through my luckless fate;
"A still lengthening life of sorrow—I henceforth must sadly lead.
"Ere his destined day none dieth—this of aged seers the lore;
"Therefore am not I too trampled—by this herd of furious beasts.
"Every deed of living mortal—by over-ruling fate is done.
"Yet no sin have I committed—in my blameless infancy,

"To deserve this dire disaster—or in word, or deed, or thought.
"For the choosing of my husband—are the guardians of the world,
"Angry are the gods, rejected—for the noble Nala's sake?
"From my lord this long divorcement—through their power do I endure."
Thus the noblest of all women—to bewail her fate began,
The deserted Damayanti—with these sad and bitter words;
With some Veda-reading Brahmins—that survived that scattered host,
Then she went her way in sadness—like the young moon's sickle pale,
And ere long a mighty city—that afflicted queen drew near:
'Twas the king of Chedi's city—truth-discerning Subahu.
Scantly clad in half a garment—entered she that stately town;
Her disturbed, emaciate, wretched—with dishevelled hair, unwashed,
Like a maniac, onward-moving—saw that city's wondering throng;
Gazing on her as she entered—to the monarch's royal seat;
All the boys her footsteps followed—in their curious gamesome play;
Circled round by these she wandered—near the royal palace gate.
From that palace lofty terrace—her the mother of the king
Saw, and thus her nurse addressed she—"Go, and lead that wanderer in!
"Sad she roves, without a refuge—troubled by those gazing men;
"Yet in form so bright, irradiate—is our palace where she moves.
"Though so maniac-like, half-clothed—like Heaven's long-eyed queen she
"seems."
She those crowding men dispersing—quickly to the palace top
Made her mount—and in amazement—her the mother-queen addressed:
"Thus though bowed and worn with sorrow—such a shining form thou wear'st,
"As through murky clouds the lightning—tell me who thou art and whence:
"For thy form is more than human—of all ornament despoiled:
"Men thou fear'st not, unattended—in celestial beauty safe."

Hearing thus her gentle language—Bhima's daughter made reply,
" Know me like thyself a mortal—a distressed, devoted wife ;
" Of illustrious race an handmaid—making where I will mine home ;
" On the roots and wild-fruits feeding—lonely, at the fall of eve.
" Gifted with unnumber'd virtues—is my true, my faithful lord,
" And I still the hero followed—like his shadow on the way.
" 'Twas his fate, with desp'rate fondness—to pursue the love of play,
" And in play subdued and ruined—entered he yon lonely wood ;
" Him, arrayed in but one garment,—like a madman wandering wild,
" To console my noble husband—I too entered the deep wood ;
" He within that dreary forest—for some cause, to me unknown,
" Wild with hunger, reft of reason—that one single robe he lost.
" I with but one robe, him naked—frantic, and with mind diseased,
" Following through the boundless forest—many a night I had not slept;
" Then, when I had sunk to slumber—me the blameless leaving there,
" Half my garment having severed—he his sinless consort fled ;
" Seeking him, my outcast husband—night and day am I consumed:
" Him I see not, ever shining—like the lotus cup, beloved ;
" Find him not, most like th' immortals—lord of all, my life, my soul."
Even as thus, with eyes o'erflowing—uttered she her sad lament,
Sad herself, sad Bhima's daughter—did the mother queen address:
" Dwell with me, then, noble Lady—deep the joy in thee I feel,
" And the servants of my household—shall thy royal husband seek ;
" Haply hither he may wander—as he roams about the world:
" Dwelling here in peace and honour—thou thy husband wilt rejoin."
To the king of Chedi's mother—Damayanti made reply ;
" On these terms, O nurse of heroes!—I with thee may make abode:
" That I eat not broken victuals—wash not feet with menial hand:

"Nor with stranger men have converse—in my chaste, secluded state;
"If that any man demand me—be he punished; if again,
"Be he put to death on th' instant—this the vow that I have sworn.
"Only, if they seek my husband—holy Brahmins will I see.
"Be my terms by thee accepted—gladly will I sojourn here,
"But on other terms no sojourn—will this heart resolved admit."
Then to her with joyful spirit—spake the mother of the king:
"As thou wilt shall all be ordered—be thou blest, since such thy vow."
Speaking thus to Bhima's daughter—did the royal mother then,
In these words address her daughter—young Sunanda was her name:
"See this handmaid, my Sunanda—gifted with a form divine;
"She in age thy lovely compeer—be she to thee as a friend;
"Joined with her in sweet communion—take thy pleasure without fear."
Young Sunanda, all rejoicing—to her own abode went back,
Taking with her Damayanti—circled with her virgin peers.

BOOK XIV.

DAMAYANTI when deserting—royal Nala fled, ere long
Blazing in the forest jungle—he a mighty fire beheld;
Thence as of a living being—from the midst a voice he heard:
"Hasten, Nala!" oft and loudly—"Punyasloka, haste," it cried.
"Fear thou not," king Nala answered—plunging in the ruddy flame;
There he saw the king of serpents—lying, coiled into a ring.
There with folded hands the serpent—trembling, thus to Nala spake:
"Me, Karkotaka, the Serpent—know, thou sovereign of men;
"Nárada, the famous hermit—I deceived, the holy sage;
"He in righteous indignation—smote me with this awful curse:
"Stay thou there as one unmoving—till king Nala passing by,
"Lead thee hence; save only Nala—none can free thee from this curse.
"Through this potent execration—I no step have power to move;
"I the way to bliss will show thee—if thou sav'st me from this fate.
"I will show thee noble friendship—serpent none is like to me;
"Lightly shall I weigh, uplift me—in thy hand, with speed, O king."
Thus when spake the king of serpents—to a finger's size he shrank;
Him when Nala lightly lifted—to the unburning space he passed.
To the air all cool and temperate—brought him, by the flame unreached.
As he fain on th' earth would place him—thus Karkotaka began.
"Move thou now, O king, and slowly—as thou movest, count thy steps.
"Then the best of all good fortune—will I give thee, mighty armed!"
Ere the tenth step he had counted—him the sudden serpent bit:
As he bit him, on the instant—all his kingly form was changed.

H

There he stood, and gazed in wonder—Nala, on his altered form.
In his proper shape the serpent—saw the sovereign of men.
Then Karkotaka the serpent—thus to Nala comfort spake:
"Through my power thy form is altered—lest thou should'st be known of men.
"He through whom thou'rt thus afflicted—Nala, with intensest grief,
"Through my poison, shall in anguish—ever dwell within thy soul.
"All his body steeped in poison—till he free thee from thy woe,
"Shall he dwell within thee prison'd—in the ecstacy of pain.
"So from him, by whom, thou blameless!—sufferest such unworthy wrong,
"By the curse I lay upon him—my deliverance shall be wrought.
"Fear not thou the tusked wild boar—foeman fear not thou, O king,
"Neither Brahmin fear, nor Sages—safe through my prevailing power.
"King, this salutary poison—gives to thee nor grief nor pain;
"In the battle, chief of Rajas—victory is ever thine.
"Go thou forth, thyself thus naming—Vahuca, the charioteer,
"To the royal Rituparna—in the dice all-skilful he;
"To Ayodhya's pleasant city—sovereign of Nishadha! go;
"He his skill in dice will give thee—for thy skill in taming steeds:
"Of Ikshwàku's noble lineage—he will be thy best of friends.
"Thou the skill in dice possessing—soon wilt rise again to bliss;
"With thy consort reunited—yield not up thy soul to grief.
"Thou thy kingdom, thou thy children—wilt regain, the truth I speak.
"When again thou would'st behold thee—in thy proper form, O king,
"Summon me to thy remembrance—and this garment put thou on:
"In this garment clad resum'st thou—instantly thy proper form."
Saying thus, of vests celestial—gave he to the king a pair.
And king Nala, thus instructed—gifted with these magic robes,
Instantly the king of serpents—vanished from his sight away.

BOOK XV

VANISHED thus the King of Serpents—set Nishadha's raja forth,
Rituparna's royal city—on the tenth day entered he.
Straight before the royal presence—"Vahuca am I," he said,
"In the skill of taming horses—on the earth is not my peer;
"Use me, where the difficult counsel—where thou want'st the dexterous
"hand;
"In the art of dressing viands—I am skilful above all.
"Whatsoe'er the art, whatever—be most difficult to do,
"I will strive to execute it—take me to thy service, king."

ITUPARN A *spake*.

"Vahuca, I bid thee welcome—all this service shalt thou do,
"On my horses' rapid motion—deeply is my mind engaged.
"Take thou then on thee the office—that my steeds be fleet of foot,
"Of my horse be thou the master—hundred hundreds is thy pay:
"Ever shalt thou have for comrades—Varshneya and Jivala:
"With these two pursue thy pleasure—Vahuca, abide with me."
Thus addressed, did Nala, honoured—by king Rituparna long,
With Varshneya in that city—and with Jivala abide:
There abode he, sadly thinking—of Vidarbha's daughter still.
In the evening, every evening—uttered he this single verse;
"Where is she, by thirst and hunger—worn, and weary, pious still,
"Thinking of her unwise husband—in whose presence is she now?"
Thus the raja, ever speaking—Jivala one night addressed;

"Who is she, for whom thou grievest?—Vahuca, I fain would hear."
Answered thus the royal Nala—"To a man of sense bereft,
"Once belonged a peerless lady—most infirm of word was he;
"From some cause from her dissevered—went that frantic man away,
"In his foolish soul thus parted—wanders he, by sorrow racked;
"Night and day, and still for ever—by his parching grief consumed:
"Nightly brooding o'er his sorrows—sings he this sad single verse.
"O'er the whole wide earth a wanderer—chance-alighting in some place,
"Dwells that woful man, unworthy,—ever wakeful with his grief.
"Him that noble lady following—in the forest lone and dread,
"Lives, of that bad man forsaken—hard it is to say, she lives!
"Lone, and young, the ways unknowing—undeserving of such fate,
"Pines she there with thirst and hunger—hard it is to say, she lives.
"In that vast and awful forest—haunted by fierce beasts of prey,
"By her lord she roams forsaken—hapless, by that luckless lord."
Thus remembering Damayanti—did Nishadha's king unknown,
Long within that dwelling sojourn—in the palace of the king.

BOOK XVI.

NALA thus bereft of kingdom—with his wife to slavery sunk,
Forth king Bhima sent the Brahmins—Nala through the world to seek.
Thus the royal Bhima charged them—with abundant wealth supplied:—
" Go ye now and seek king Nala—Damayanti seek, my child:
" And, achieved this weighty business—found Nishadha's royal lord,
" Whosoe'er shall hither bring them—shall a thousand kine receive;
" And a royal grant for maintenance—of a village like a town.
" If nor hither Damayanti—nor king Nala may be brought,
" Know we where they are, rich guerdon—still we give, ten hundred kine."
Thus addressed, the joyful Brahmins—went to every clime of earth,
Through the cities, through the kingdoms—seeking Nala and his queen:
Nala, or king Bhima's daughter—in no place might they behold.
Then a Brahmin, named Sudeva—came to pleasant Chedi-pur;
There within the kingly palace—he Vidarbha's daughter saw,
Standing with the fair Sunanda—on a royal holiday.
With her beauty once so peerless—worthy now of little praise,
Like the sun-light feebly shining—through the dimness of a cloud.
Gazing on the large-eyed princess—dull in look, and wasted still,
Lo, he thought, king Bhima's daughter—pondering thus within his mind.—

SUDEVA *spake.*

" Even as once I wont to see her—such is yonder woman's form,
I my work have done, beholding—like the goddess world-adored,
Like the full moon, darkly beauteous—with her fair and swelling breasts,
Her, the queen, that with her brightness—makes each clime devoid of gloom,

With her lotus eyes expanding—like Manmatha's queen divine;
Like the moonlight in its fulness—the desire of all the world.
From Vidarbha's pleasant waters—her by cruel fate plucked up,
Like a lotus flower uprooted—with the mire and dirt around:
Like the pallid night, when Rahu—swallows up the darkened moon:
For her husband wan with sorrow—like a gentle stream dried up;
Like a pool, where droops the lotus—whence the affrighted birds have fled,
By the elephant's proboscis—in its quiet depths disturbed.
Tender, soft-limbed, in a palace—fit, of precious stones, to dwell.
Like the lotus stem, uprooted—parched and withered by the sun.
Fair in form, in soul as generous—worthy of all bliss, unbless'd,
Like the young moon's slender crescent—in the heavens by dark clouds veiled
Widowed now of all love's pleasures—of her noble kin despoiled,
Wretched, bearing life, her husband—in her hope again to see.
To the unadorned, a husband—is the chiefest ornament;
Of her husband if forsaken—she in splendour is not bright.
Difficult must be the trial—does king Nala, reft of her,
Still retain his wretched body—nor with sorrow pine away?
Her with her dark flowing tresses—with her long and lotus eyes,
Worthy of all joy, thus joyless—as I see, my soul is wrung.
To the furthest shore of sorrow—when will pass this beauteous queen?
To her husband reunited—as the moon's bride to the moon?
Her recovering shall king Nala—to his happiness return,
King, albeit despoiled of kingdom—he his realm shall reassume;
In their age and virtues equal—equal in their noble race,
He alone of her is worthy—worthy she alone of him.
Me beseems it of that peerless—of that brave and prudent king,
To console the loyal consort—pining for her husband's sight.

Her will I address with comfort—with her moonlike glowing face.
Her with woe once unacquainted—woful now and lost in thought."
Thus when he had gazed and noted—all her marks, her features well,
To the daughter of king Bhima—thus the sage Sudeva spake:
"I am named Sudeva, lady—I, thy brother's chosen friend,
"By king Bhima's royal mandate—hither come in search of thee.
"Well thy sire, thy royal mother—well thy noble brethren fare,
"And well fare those little infants—well and happy are they both.
"For thy sake thy countless kindred—sit as though of sense bereft:
"Seeking thee a hundred Brahmins—now are wandering o'er the earth."
She no sooner knew Sudeva—Damayanti, of her kin,
Many a question asked in order—and of every friend beloved.
And the daughter of Vidarbha—freely wept, so sudden thus
On Sudeva, best of Brahmins—gazing, on her brother's friend.
Her beheld the young Sunanda—weeping, wasted with distress,
As she thus her secret converse—with the wise Sudeva held.
Thus she spake unto her mother—"Lo, how fast our handmaid weeps,
Since her meeting with the Brahmin—who she is, thou now may'st know."
Forth the king of Chedi's mother—from the inner chamber went,
And she passed where with the Brahmin—that mysterious woman stood.
Them the mother queen Sudeva—bade before her presence stand;
And she asked, "Whose wife, whose daughter—may this noble stranger be?
"From her kindred how dissevered—from her husband, the soft-eyed?
"Is she known to thee, O Brahmin—canst thou tell from whence she came?
"This I fain would hear, and clearly—all her strange and wonderous tale.
"Tell me all that hath befallen—to this heaven-formed, plainly tell."
Best of Brahmins, thus Sudeva—by the mother queen addressed,
All the truth of Damayanti—sitting at his ease, declared.

BOOK XVII.

"In Vidarbha the just monarch—Bhima, in his glory dwells.
"Of that king is she the daughter—Damayanti is her name;
"And the raja of Nishadha—Nala, Virasena's son,
"Of that king is she the consort—Punyasloka named, the Wise.
"Him in play his brother worsted—spoiled of realm the king of earth:
"He set forth with Damayanti—whither is unknown of men.
"For the sake of Damayanti—wander we about the earth;
"Till I found yon noble woman—in the palace of your son.
"Like to her of mortal women—is there none, her beauty's peer;
"In the midst, between her eyebrows—from her birth a lovely mole,
"Dark was seen, and like a lotus—that hath vanished from my sight,
"Covered over with defilement—like the moon behind a cloud.
"This soft mark of perfect beauty—fashioned thus by Brahma's self,
"As at change the moon's thin crescent—only dim and faintly gleams.
"Yet her beauty is not faded—clouded o'er with toil and mire
"Though she be, it shines apparent, like the native unwrought gold.
"With that beauteous form yon woman—gifted with that lovely mole,
"Instant knew I for the Princess—as the heat betrays the fire."

Vrihadasva *spake.*

To Sudeva as she listened—uttering thus his strange discourse:
"All the dust that mole concealing—young Sunanda washed away.
"By the obscuring dust unclouded—shining out that mole appeared;
"On the brow of Damayanti—like the unclouded moon in heaven.

Gazing on that mole, Sunanda—and the mother of the king,
Wept as fondly they embraced her—and an instant silent stood.
Then her tears awhile suppressing—thus the royal mother spake:
"Thou art mine own sister's daughter—by that beauteous mole made known;
"I, Oh beauteous, and thy mother—of that lofty-minded king,
"Are the daughters, king Sudaman—he that in Dasarna reigns;
"She was wedded to king Bhima—and to Viravahu I.
"In my father's home, Dasarna—once I saw thee, newly born.
"As to me thy father's lineage—is akin, so mine to thee;
"Whatsoe'er my power commandeth—Damayanti, all is thine."
To the queen did Damayanti—in the gladness of her heart,
Having bowed in courteous homage—to her mother's sister, speak:
"While unknown I might continue—gladly dwelt I here with thee;
"Every want supplied on th' instant—guarded by thy gentle care.
"Yet than even this pleasent dwelling—a more pleasant may there be;
"Long a banished woman, mother!—give me leave from hence to part,
"Thither where my infant children—dwell my tender little ones,
"Orphaned of their sire, in sorrow—orphaned, ah, how long of me!
"If thou yet wilt grant a favour—o'er all other favours dear,
"To Vidarbha would I journey—quick the palanquin command."
"Be it so," her mother's sister—joyful, instant made reply.
Guarded by a mighty army—with th' approval of her son,
Sent the queen, that happy lady—in a palanquin, by men
Borne aloft, and well provided—with all raiment, drink, and food.
Thus the princess to Vidarbha—after brief delay returned.
Her her whole assembled kindred—welcomed home with pride and joy,
All in health she found her kinsmen—and that lovely infant pair,
With her mother, with her father—and her sister troop of friends.

To the gods she paid her worship—to the Brahmins in her joy;
So the queenly Damayanti—all in noblest guise performed.
And her royal sire Sudeva—with the thousand kine made glad,
Joyous to behold his daughter,—with a village and much wealth.
There, when in her father's palace—she the quiet night had passed,
In these words the noble lady—to her mother gan to speak:
"If in life thou would'st preserve me—mother, hear the truth I speak;
"Home to bring the hero Nala—be it now thy chiefest toil."
Thus addressed by Damayanti—very sorrowful the queen
Clouded all her face with weeping—not a word in answer spake.
But the princess, thus afflicted—when the female train beheld,
"Woe! oh woe!" they shrieked together—all in pitying sadness wept.
To the mighty raja Bhima—did the queen that speech relate.
"'Damayanti, Lo thy daughter—for her husband sits and mourns.'
"Breaking through all bashful silence—thus, oh king, to me she spake:
"'Be it now thy servants' business—to find out the king of men.'"
Urged by her the king his Brahmins—to his will obedient all,
Sent around to every region—"Be your care the king to find."
Then those Brahmins at the mandate—of Vidarbha's royal lord,
First drew near to Damayanti—"Lo, now set we forth," they said.
Then to them spake Bhima's daughter—"In all realms be this your speech,
"Wheresoever men assemble—this repeat again, again:
"Whither went'st thou then, oh gamester!—half my garment severing off,
"Leaving me within the forest—all forsaken, thy beloved.
"Even as thou commandedst, sits she—sadly waiting thy return.
"Parched with sorrow sits that woman—in her scant half garment glad.
"Oh to her thus ever weeping—in the extreme of her distress,
"Grant thy pity, noble hero—answer to her earnest prayer.

"Be this also said, to move him—to compassionate my state,
"(By the wind within the forest—fanned, intensely burns the fire).
"Ever by her consort cherished—and sustained the wife should be.
"Why hast thou forgot that maxim—thou in every duty skilled.
"Thou wert ever called the generous—thou the gentle and the wise.
"Art thou now estranged from pity—through my sad injurious fate.
"Prince of men, O grant thy pity—grant it, lord of men, to me;
"'Mercy is the chief of duties,'—oft from thine own lips I've heard.
"Thus as ye are ever speaking—should there any one reply,
"Mark him well, lest he be Nala—who he is, and where he dwells.
"He who to this speech hath listened—and hath thus his answer made,
"Be his words, O best of Brahmins—treasured and brought home to me,
"Lest he haply should discover—that by my command ye speak,
"That again ye may approach him—do ye this without delay.
"Whether he be of the wealthy—whether of the poor he be;
"Be he covetous of riches—learn ye all he would desire."
Thus addressed, went forth the Brahmins—to the realms on every side,
Seeking out the royal Nala—in his dark concealed distress.
They through royal cities, hamlets—pastoral dwellings, hermits' cells,
Nala every-where went seeking—yet those Brahmins found him not.
All in every part went speaking—in the language they were taught;
In the words of Damayanti—spake they in the ears of men.

BOOK XVIII.

Long the time that passed, a Brahmin—wise Parnada was his name,
Home returning to the city—thus to Bhima's daughter spake:
"Damayanti! royal Nala—as I sought Nishadha's king,
"Came I to Ayodhya's city—the Bhangasuri's abode.
"Stood before me, eager listening—to the words thou bad'st us speak,
"He, the prosperous Rituparna—all excelling! such his name.
"Thus as spake I, answered nothing—Rituparna, king of men;
"Nor of all that full assemblage—more than once addressed by me.
"By the king dismissed, when sate I—in a solitary place,
"One of Rituparna's household—Vahuca, his name, drew near,
"Charioteer of that great raja—with short arms and all deformed,
"Skilled to drive the rapid chariot—skilled the viands to prepare.
"He, when much he'd groaned in anguish—and had wept again, again,
"First his courteous salutation—made, then spake in words like these:
"Even in the extreme of misery—noble women still preserve,
"Over their ownselves the mastery—by their virtues winning heaven;
"Of their faithless lords abandoned—anger feel not even then.
"In the breastplate of their virtue—noble women live unharmed.
"By the wretched, by the senseless—by the lost to every joy,
"She by such a lord forsaken—yet to anger will not yield.
"Against him his sustenance seeking—of his robe by birds despoiled,
"Him consumed with utmost misery—still no wrath the dark-hued feels;

"Treated well, or ill entreated—when her husband she beholds,
"Spoiled of bliss, bereft of kingdom—famine-wasted, worn with woe.
"Having heard the stranger's language—hither hasted I to come.
"Thou hast heard, be thine the judgment—to the king relate thou all."
To Parnada having listened—with her eyes o'erflowed with tears,
Secretly went Damayanti—and her mother thus addressed:
"Let not what I speak to Bhima—O my mother, be made known—
"In thy presence to Sudeva—best of Brahmins, I would speak.
"Let not this my secret counsel—to king Bhima be disclosed;
"This the object we must compass—if thy daughter thou wouldst please,
"As myself was to my kindred—swiftly by Sudeva brought,
"With the same good fortune swiftly—may Sudeva part from hence,
"Home to bring the royal Nala—mother, to Ayodhya's town."
Resting from his toil, Parnada—of the Brahmin race the best,
Did the daughter of Vidarbha—honour, and with wealth reward.
"Brahmin! home if come my Nala—richer guerdon will I give;
"Much hast thou achieved, and wisely—so as none but thou has done.
"That again with my lost husband—noblest Brahmin, I may meet."
Thus addressed, his grateful homage—and his benedictions paid,
Having thus achieved his mission—home the wise Parnada went.
Then accosting good Sudeva—Damayanti thus began,
And before her mother's presence—in her pain and grief she spake:
"Go, Sudeva, to the city—where Ayodhya's raja dwells,
"Speak thou thus to Rituparna—Come, as of thine own accord.
"Once again her Swayembara—does king Bhima's daughter hold;
"Damayanti, thither hasten—all the kings and sons of kings;
"Closely now the time is reckoned—when to-morrow's dawn appears;
"If that thou would'st win the Princess—speed thou, tamer of thy foes.

"When the sun is in his rising—she a second lord will choose:
"Whether lives or is not living—royal Nala, no one knows."
Thus, as he received his mission—hastening to the king, he spake,
To the royal Rituparna—spake Sudeva, in these words.

BOOK XIX.

HEARING thus Sudeva's language—Ritupurna, king of men
With a gentle voice and blandly—thus to Vahuca began.
"Where the princess Damayanti—doth her Swayembara hold
"In one day to far Vidarbha—Vahuca, I fain would go."
In these words the unknown Nala—by his royal lord addressed
All his heart was torn with anguish—thus the lofty-minded thought—
"Can she speak thus, Damayanti—thus with sorrow frantic act?
"Is't a stratagem thus subtly—for my sake devised and plann'd?
"To desire this deed unholy—is that holy princess driven
"Wrong'd by me, her basest husband—miserable, mind-estranged!
"Fickle is the heart of woman—grievous too is my offence!
"Hence she thus might act ignobly—in her exile, reft of friends,
"Soul-disturbed by her great sorrow—in the excess of her despair.
"No! she could not thus have acted—she with noble offspring blest.
"Where the truth, and where the falsehood—setting forth, I best shall judge,
"I the will of Rituparna—for mine own sake, will obey."
Thus within his mind revolving—Vahuca, his wretched mind,
With his folded hands addressed he—Rituparna, king of men:
"I thy mandate will accomplish—I will go, O king of men,
"In a single day, O raja—to Vidarbha's royal town."
Vahuca of all the coursers—did a close inspection make
Entering in the royal stable—by Bhangasuri's command.
Ever urged by Rituparna—Vahuca, in horses skilled,
Long within himself debating—which the fleetest steeds to choose,

He approached four slender coursers—fit, and powerful for the road,
Blending mighty strength with fleetness—high in courage and in blood;
Free from all the well-known vices—broad of nostril—large of jaw;
With the ten good marks distinguished—born in Sindhu—fleet as wind.
As he gazed upon those coursers—spoke the king, almost in wrath:
"Is then thus fulfilled our mandate?—think not to deceive us so.
"How will these my coursers bear us—slight in strength and slightly
"breathed—
"How can such a way be travelled—and so long, by steeds like these?"—

VAHUCA *spake.*

"Two on th' head, one on the forehead—two and two on either flank—
"Two, behold, the chest discloses—and upon the crupper one—
"These the horses to Vidharba—that will bear us, doubt not thou;
"Yet, if others thou preferest—speak, and I will yoke them straight."

RITUPARNA *spake.*

"In the knowledge thou of horses—Vahuca, hast matchless skill;
"Whichso'er thou think'st the fittest—harness thou without delay."

Then those four excelling horses—nobly bred—of courage high,
In their harness to the chariot—did the skilful Nala yoke.—
To the chariot yoked, as mounted—in his eager haste the king
To the earth those best of horses—bowed their knees and stooped them down.
Then the noblest of all heroes—Nala, with a soothing voice,
Spake unto those horses, gifted—both with fleetness and with strength.
Up the reins when he had gathered—he the charioteer bade mount,
First, Varshneya, skilled in driving—at full speed then set he forth.

Urged by Vahuca, those coursers—to the utmost of their speed,
All at once in th' air sprung upward—as the driver to unseat.
Then, as he beheld those horses—bearing him as fleet as wind,
Did the monarch of Ayodhya—in his silent wonder sit.
When the rattling of the chariot—when the guiding of the reins,
When of Vahuca the science—saw he, thus Varshneya thought:
"Is it Matali, the chariot—of the king of heaven that drives?
"Lo, in Vahuca each virtue—of that godlike charioteer!
"Is it Salihotra skilful—in the race, the strength of steeds,
"That hath ta'en a human body—thus all-glorious to behold?
"Is't, or can it be, king Nala—conqueror of his foemen's realms?
"Is the lord of men before us?"—thus within himself he thought.
"If the skill possessed by Nala—Vahuca possesseth too,
"Lo, of Vahuca the knowledge—and of Nala equal seems;
"And of Vahuca and Nala—thus alike the age should be.
"If 'tis not the noble Nala—it is one of equal skill.
"Mighty ones, disguised, are wandering—in the precincts of this earth.
"They, divine by inborn nature—but in earthly forms concealed.
"His deformity of body—that my judgment still confounds;
"Yet that proof alone is wanting—what shall then my judgment be?
"In their age they still are equal—though unlike that form misshaped,
"Nala gifted with all virtues—Vahuca I needs must deem."
Thus the charioteer Varshneya—sate debating in his mind;
Much, and much again he pondered—in the silence of his thought.
But the royal Rituparna—Vahuca's surpassing skill,
With the charioteer Varshneya—sate admiring, and rejoiced.
In the guiding of the coursers—his attentive hand he watched,
Wondered at his skill, consummate—in consummate joy himself.

K

BOOK XX.

Over rivers, over mountains—through the forests, over lakes,
Fleetly passed they, rapid gliding—like a bird along the air.
As the chariot swiftly travelled—lo, Bhangasuri the king
Saw his upper garment fallen—from the lofty chariot seat;
Though in urgent haste, no sooner—he his fallen mantle saw,
Than the king exclaimed to Nala—"Pause, and let us take it up:
"Check, an instant, mighty-minded!—check thy fiery-footed steeds,
"While Varshneya, swift dismounting—bears me back my fallen robe."
Nala answered, "Far behind us—doth thy fallen garment lie;
"Ten miles, lo, it lies behind us—turn we not, to gain it, back."
Answered thus by noble Nala—then Bhangasuri the king,
Bowed with fruit, within the forest—saw a tall Vibhitak tree:
Gazing on that tree, the raja—spake to Vahuca in haste,
"Now, O charioteer, in numbers, thou shalt see my passing skill.
"Each one knows not every science—none there is that all things knows:
"Perfect skill in every knowledge—in one mind there may not be.
"On yon tree are leaves how many?—Vahuca, how many fruit?
"Say, how many are there fallen?—one above a hundred, there.
"One leaf is there 'bove a hundred—and one fruit, O Vahuca!
"And of leaves are five ten millions—hanging on those branches two.
"Those two branches if thou gather—and the twigs that on them grow,
"On those two are fruits two thousand—and a hundred, less by five."
Then, when he had check'd the chariot—answered Vahuca the king,
"What thou speakest, to mine eyesight—all invisible appears;

" Visible I'll make it, counting—on yon boughs the leaves and fruit :"
" Then, when we have strictly numbered—I mistrust mine eyes no more.
" In thy presence, king, I'll number—yonder tall Vibhitak-tree.
" Whether it may be, or may not—this not done, I cannot know.
" I will number, thou beholding—all its fruits, O king of men,
" But an instant let Varshneya—hold the bridles of the steeds."
To the charioteer the raja—answered, " Time is none to stay."
Vahuca replied, all eager—his own purpose to fulfil,
" Either stay thou here an instant—or go onward in thy speed,
" With the charioteer Varshneya—go, for straight the road before."
Answered him king Rituparna—with a bland and soothing voice :
" Charioteer ! on earth thine equal—Vahuca, there may not be ;
" By thy guidance, skilled in horses !—to Vidarbha I would go :
" I in thee have placed reliance—interrupt not then our course :
" Willingly will I obey thee—Vahuca, in what thou ask'st,
" If this day we reach Vidarbha—ere the sun hath sunk in night."
Vahuca replied, " No sooner—have I numbered yonder fruit,
" To Vidarbha will I hasten—grant me then my prayer, O king."
Then the raja, all reluctant—" Stay then, and begin to count ;
" Of one branch one part, O blameless—from the tall Vibhitak tree,
" Man of truth, begin to number—and make glad thine inmost heart."
From the chariot quick alighting—Nala tore the branch away.
Then, his soul possess'd with wonder—to the raja thus he said ;
" Having counted, as thou sawest—even so many fruits there are,
" Marvellous thy power, O monarch—by mine eyes beheld and proved,
" Of that wonder-working science—fain the secret would I hear."
Then the raja spake in answer—eager to pursue his way,
" I of dice possess the science—and in numbers thus am skilled."

Vahuca replied; "That science—if to me thou wilt impart,
"In return, O king, receive thou—my surpassing skill in steeds."
Then the raja Rituparna—by his pressing need induced,
Eager for that skill in horses—"Be it so," thus 'gan to say;
"Well, O Vahuca, thou speakest—thou my skill in dice receive,
"And of steeds thy wondrous knowledge—be to me a meet return."
Rituparna, all his science—saying this, to Nala gave.
Soon as he in dice grew skilful—Kali from his body passed:
He Karkotaka's foul poison—vomiting from out his mouth,
Went from forth his body Kali—tortured by that fiery curse.
Nala, wasted by that conflict—came not instant to himself,
But, released from that dread venom—Kali his own form resumed:
And Nishadha's monarch, Nala—fain would curse him in his ire.
Him addressed the fearful Kali—trembling, and with folded hands;
"Lord of men, restrain thine anger—I will give thee matchless fame;
"Indrasena's wrathful mother—laid on me her fatal curse,
"When by thee she was deserted—since that time, O king of men,
"I have dwelt in thee in anguish—in the ecstacy of pain.
"By the King of Serpents' poison—I have burned by night, by day;
"To thy mercy now for refuge—flee I, hear my speech, O king:
"Wheresoe'er men, unforgetful—through the world shall laud thy name,
"Shall the awful dread of Kali—never in their soul abide.
"If thou wilt not curse me, trembling—and to thee for refuge fled."
Thus addressed, the royal Nala—all his rising wrath suppressed,
And the fearful Kali entered—in the cloven Vibhitak tree:
To no eyes but those of Nala—visible, had Kali spoken.
Then the monarch of Nishadha—from his inward fever freed,
When away had vanished Kali—when the fruits he had numbered all,

Triumphing in joy unwonted—blazing in his splendour forth,
Proudly mounting on the chariot—onward urged the rapid steeds.
But that tree by Kali entered—since that time stands aye accursed.
Those fleet horses, forward flying—like to birds, again, again,
All his soul elate with transport—Nala swifter, swifter drove ;
With his face towards Vidarbha—rode the raja in his pride :
And when forward Nala journeyed—Kali to his home returned.
So released from all his sufferings—Nala went, the king of men,
Dispossessed by Kali, wanting—only now his proper form.

BOOK XXI.

WITH the evening in Vidarbha—men at watch, as they drew near,
Mighty Rituparna's coming—to king Bhima did proclaim.
Then that king, by Bhima's mandate—entered in Kundina's walls,
All the region round him echoing—with the thunders of his car.
But the echoing of that chariot—when king Nala's horses heard,
In their joy they pawed and trampled—even as Nala's self were there.
Damayanti, too, the rushing—of king Nala's chariot heard.
As a cloud that hoarsely thunders—at the coming of the rains.
All her heart was thrilled with wonder—at that old familiar sound.
On they seemed to come, as Nala—drove of yore his trampling steeds:
Like it seemed to Bhima's daughter—and e'en so to Nala's steeds.
On the palace roofs the peacocks—th' elephants within their stalls,
And the horses heard the rolling—of the mighty monarch's car.
Elephants and peacocks hearing—the fleet chariot rattling on,
Up they raised their necks and clamoured—as at sound of coming rain.

DAMAYANTI *spake.*

"How the rolling of yon chariot—filling, as it seems, th' earth,
"Thrills my soul with unknown transport—it is Nala, king of men.
"If this day I see not Nala—with his glowing moonlike face,
"Him, the king with countless virtues—I shall perish without doubt.
"If this day within th' embraces—of that hero's clasping arms,
"I the gentle pressure feel not—without doubt I shall not live.
"If 'tis not, like cloud of thunder—he that comes, Nishadha's king,

"I this day the fire will enter—burning like the hue of gold.
"In his might like the strong lion—like the raging elephant,
"Comes he not, the prince of princes—I shall perish without doubt.
"Not a falsehood I remember—I remember no offence;
"Not an idle word remember—in his noble converse free.
"Lofty, patient, like a hero—liberal beyond all kings,
"Nought ignoble, as the eunuch—even in private, may he do.
"As I think upon his virtues—as I think by day, by night,
"All my heart is rent with anguish—widowed of its own beloved."
Thus lamenting, she ascended—as with frenzied mind possessed,
To the palace roof's high terrace—to behold the king of men.
In the middle court high seated—in the car, the lord of earth,
Rituparna with Varshneya—and with Vahuca she saw,
When Varshneya from that chariot—and when Vahuca came down,
He let loose those noble coursers—and he stopped the glowing car.
From that chariot-seat descended—Rituparna, king of men,
To the noble monarch Bhima—he drew near, for strength renowned.
Him received with highest honour—Bhima, for without due cause,
Deemed not he, the mighty raja—with such urgent speed had come.
"Wherefore com'st thou! hail and welcome"—thus that gracious king enquires;
For his daughter's sake he knew not—that the lord of men had come.
But the raja Rituparna—great in wisdom as in might,
When nor king within the palace—nor king's son he could behold,
Nor of Swayembara heard he—nor assembled Brahmins saw.
Thus within his mind deep pondering—spoke of Kosala the lord.
"Hither, O majestic Bhima—to salute thee am I come."
But king Bhima smiled in secret—as he thought within his mind,

"What the cause of this far journey—of a hundred Yojanas.
"Passing through so many cities—for this cause he set not forth;
"For this cause of little moment—to our court he hath not come:
"What the real cause, hereafter—haply I may chance to know."
After royal entertainment—then the king his guest dismissed:
"Take then thy repose," thus said he—"weary of thy journey, rest."
He refreshed, with courteous homage—of that courteous king took leave,
Ushered by the royal servants—to th' appointed chamber went:
There retired king Rituparna—with Varshneya in his suite.
Vahuca, meantime, the chariot—to the chariot-house had led,
There the coursers he unharnessed—skilfully he dressed them there,
And with gentle words caressed them—on the chariot seat sate down.

But the woeful Damayanti—when Bhangasuri she'd seen,
And the charioteer Varshneya—and the seeming Vahuca,
Thought within Vidarbha's princess—"Whose was that fleet chariot's sound?
"Such it seems as noble Nala's—yet no Nala do I see.
"Hath the charioteer Varshneya—Nala's noble science learned?
"Therefore did the thundering chariot—sound as driven by Nala's self?
"Or may royal Rituparna—like the skilful Nala drive,
"Therefore did the rolling chariot—seem as of Nishadha's king?"
Thus when Damayanti pondered—in the silence of her soul,
Sent she then her beauteous handmaid—to that king her messenger.

BOOK XXII.

DAMAYANTI *spake.*

" Go, Kesinia, go, enquire thou—who is yonder charioteer,
" On the chariot seat reposing—all deformed, with arms so short?
" Blessed maid, approach, and courteous—open thou thy bland discourse:
" Undespis'd, ask thou thy question—and the truth let him reply.
" Much and sorely do I doubt me—whether Nala it may be,
" As my bosom's rapture augurs—as the gladness of my heart.
" Speak thou, ere thou close the converse—even as good Parnada spake,
" And his answer, slender-waisted—undespis'd, remember thou."
Then to Vahuca departing—went that zealous messenger,
On the palace' loftiest terrace—Damayanti sate and gazed.

KESINIA *spake.*

" Happy omen mark thy coming—I salute thee, king of men:
" Of the princess Damayanti—hear, O lord of men, the speech:
" 'From what region came ye hither—with what purpose are ye come?'
" Answer thou, as may beseem you—so Vidarbha's princess wills."

VAHUCA *spake.*

" Soon a second Swayembara, heard the king of Kosala,
" Damayanti holds: to-morrow—will it be, the Brahmin said:
" Hearing this, with fleetest coursers—that a hundred yojans' speed,
" Set he forth, the wind less rapid,—and his charioteer am I."

L

KESINIA *spake.*

" Who the third that journeys with you—who is he, and what his race?
" Of what race art thou? this office—wherefore dost thou undertake?"

VAHUCA *spake.*

" 'Tis the far-renowned Varshneya—Punyasloka's charioteer:
" He, when Nala fled an exile—to Bhangasuri retired.
" Skilful I in taming horses—and a famous charioteer.
" Rituparna's chosen driver—dresser of his food am I."

KESINIA *spake.*

" Knows the charioteer Varshneya—whither royal Nala went?
" Of his fortune hath he told thee—Vahuca, what hath he said?"

VAHUCA *spake.*

" He of the unhappy Nala—safe the children borne away,
" Wheresoe'er he would, departed—of king Nala knows he nought:
" Nothing of Nishadha's raja—fair one! living man doth know.
" Through the world, concealed, he wanders—having lost his proper form.
" Only Nala's self of Nala—knows, and his own inward soul,
" Of himself to living mortal—Nala will no sign betray."

KESINIA *spake.*

" He that to Ayodhya's city—went, the holy Brahmin first,
" Of his faithful wife these sayings—uttered once and once again;
" 'Whither went'st thou then, O gamester—half my garment severing off;
" 'Leaving her within the forest—all forsaken, thy belov'd?

" 'Even as thou commanded'st, sits she—sadly waiting thy return,
" 'Day and night, consumed with sorrow—in her scant half garment clad.
" 'O to her for ever weeping—in the extreme of her distress,
" 'Grant thy pity, noble hero—answer to her earnest prayer.'
"'Speak again the words thou uttered'st—words of comfort to her soul,
" The renowned Vidarbha's princess—fain that speech would hear again,
" When the Brahmin thus had spoken—what thou answered'st back to him,
" That again Vidarbha's princess—in the self-same words would hear."

VRIHADASVA *spake.*

Of king Nala, by the handmaid—fair Kesinia thus addressed,
All the heart was wrung with sorrow—and the eyes o'erflowed with tears.
But his anguish still suppressing—inly though consumed, the king,
With a voice half choked with weeping—thus repeated his reply.
" Even in the extreme of misery—noble women still preserve
" Over their own selves the mastery—by their virtues winning heaven;
" By their faithless lords abandoned—anger feel they not, e'en then;
" In the breastplate of their virtue—noble women live unharmed.
" By the wretched, by the senseless—by the lost to every joy,
" She by such a lord forsaken—to resentment will not yield.
" Against him, by hunger wasted—of his robe by birds despoiled,
" Him consumed with utmost misery—still no wrath, the dark-hued feels;
" Treated well, or ill-entreated—when her husband 'tis she sees,
" Spoiled of bliss, bereft of kingdom—famine wasted, worn with woe."
In these words as spake king Nala—in the anguish of his heart,
Could he not refrain from weeping—his unwilling tears burst forth.
Then departing, fair Kesinia—told to Damayanti all,
All that Vahuca had spoken—all th' emotion he betrayed.

BOOK XXIII.

HEARING this, fair Damayanti—all abandoned to her grief,
Thinking still that he was Nala—to Kesinia spake again.
" Go, Kesinia, go, examine—Vahuca, and all his acts,
" Silent take thy stand beside him—and observe whate'er he does;
" Nor, Kesinia, be there given him—fire his labours to assist:
" Neither be there given him water—in thy haste, at his demand:
" All, when thou hast well observed him—every act to me repeat,
" Every act that more than mortal—seems in Vahuca, relate."
Thus addressed by Damayanti—straight Kesinia went again,
Of the tamer of the horses—every act observed, came back;
Every act as she had seen it—she to Damayanti told:
Every more than mortal wonder—that in Vahuca appeared.

KESINIA *spake.*

" Very holy is he, never—mortal man, in all my life,
" Have I seen, or have I heard of—Damayanti, like to him.
" He drew near the lowly entrance—bowed not down his stately head;
" On the instant, as it saw him—up th' expanding portal rose.
" For the use of Rituparna—much and various viands came;
" Sent, as meet, by royal Bhima—and abundant animal food.
" These to cleanse, with meet ablution—were capacious vessels brought;
" As he looked on them, the vessels—stood, upon the instant, full.
" Then, the meet ablutions over—Vahuca went forth, and took,
" Of the withered grass a handful—held it upward to the sun:

"On the instant, brightly blazing—shone the all-consuming fire.
"Much I marvelled at the wonder—and in mute amazement stood;
"Lo, a second greater marvel—sudden burst upon my sight!
"He that blazing fire stood handling—yet unharmed, unburned, remained.
"At his will flows forth the water—at his will it sinks again.
"And another greater wonder—lady, did I there behold:
"He the flowers which he had taken—gently moulded in his hands,
"In his hands the flowers, so moulded—as with freshening life endued,
"Blossomed out with richer fragrance—stood erect upon their stems:
"All these marvels having noted—swiftly came I back to thee."

DAMAYANTI *spake.*

Damayanti when these wonders—of the king of men she heard,
Thought yet more king Nala present—thought her utmost wish achieved.
Deeming still her royal consort—in the form of Vahuca,
With a gentle voice and weeping—to Kesinia spake again:
"Go, again, Kesinia, secret—and by Vahuca unseen,
"Of those viands bring a portion—by his skilful hand prepared:"
She to Vahuca approaching—unperceived stole soft away
Of the well-cooked meat a morsel—warm she bore it in her haste,
And to Damayanti gave it—fair Kesinia, undelayed.
Of the food prepared by Nala—well the flavour did she know;
Tasting it she shrieked in transport—"Nala is yon charioteer."
Trying then a new emotion—of her mouth ablution made:
She her pair of infant children—with Kesinia sent to him.
Soon as he young Indrasena—and her little brother saw,
Up he sprang, his arms wound round them—to his bosom folding both;
When he gazed upon the children—like the children of the gods,

All his heart o'erflowed with pity—and unwilling tears broke forth.
Yet Nishadha's lord perceiving—she his strong emotion marked,
From his hold released the children—to Kesinia speaking thus:
"Oh! so like mine own twin children—was yon lovely infant pair,
"Seeing them thus unexpected—have I broken out in tears:
"If so oft thou comest hither—men some evil will suspect,
"We within this land are strangers—beauteous maiden, part in peace."

BOOK XXIV.

SEEING the profound emotion—of that wisest king of men,
Passing back in haste, Kesinia—told to Damayanti all:
Then again did Damayanti—mission to Kesinia give,
To approach her royal mother—in her haste her lord to see.
"Vahuca we've watched most closely—Nala we suspect him still;
"Only from his form we doubt him—this myself would fain behold.
"Cause him enter here, my mother—to my wishes condescend;
"Known or unknown to my father—let it be decided now."
By that handmaid thus accosted—then the queen to Bhima told
All his daughter's secret counsel—and the raja gave assent.
Instant from her sire the princess—from her mother leave obtained,
Bade them make king Nala enter—in the chamber where she dwelt.
Sudden as he gazed upon her—upon Damayanti gazed,
Nala, he was seized with anguish—and with tears his eyes o'erflowed.
And when Damayanti gazed on—Nala, thus approaching near,
With an agonizing sorrow—was the noble lady seized.
Clad, then, in a scarlet mantle—hair dishevelled, mire-defiled,
Unto Vahuca this language—Damayanti thus addressed:
"Vahuca beheld'st thou ever—an upright and noble man,
"Who departed and abandoned—in the wood, his sleeping wife?
"The beloved wife, and blameless—in the wild wood, worn with grief?
"Who was he who thus forsook her?—who but Nala, king of men?
"To the lord of earth, from folly—what offence can I have given?
"That he fled, within the forest—leaving me, by sleep oppressed?

"Openly, the gods rejected—was he chosen by me, my lord:
"Could he leave the true, the loving—her that hath his children borne!
"By the nuptial fire, in presence—of the gods, he clasped my hand,
"'I will be,' this truth he plighted—whither did he then depart?"
While all this in broken accents—sadly Damayanti spoke,
From her eyes the drops of sorrow—flowed in copious torrents down.
Those dark eyes, with vermeil corners—thus with trembling moisture dewed,
When king Nala saw, and gazed on—to the sorrowful he spake.
"Gaming that I lost my kingdom—'twas not mine own guilty deed,
"It was Kali wrought within me—hence it was I fled from thee;
"Therefore he, in th' hour of trial—smitten by thy scathing curse,
"In the wild wood as thou wanderest—grieving night and day for me,
"Kali dwelt within my body—burning with thy powerful curse,
"Ever burning, fiercer, hotter—as when fire is heaped on fire.
"He, by my religious patience—my devotion, now subdued,
"Lo! the end of all our sorrows—beautiful! is now at hand.
"I, the evil one departed, hither have made haste to come;
"For thy sake, O round-limbed! only;—other business have I none.
"Yet, O how may high-born woman—from her vowed, her plighted lord,
"Swerving, choose another husband—even as thou, O trembler, would'st?
"Over all the earth the heralds—travel by the king's command,
"'Now the daughter of king Bhima—will a second husband choose,
"'Free from every tie, as wills she—as her fancy may beseem,'
"Hearing this, came hither speeding—king Bhangasuri in haste."
Damayanti, when from Nala—heard she this his grievous charge,
With her folded hands, and trembling—thus to Nala made reply:
"Do not me, O noble-minded—of such shameless guilt suspect,
"Thou, when I the gods rejected—Nala, wert my chosen lord.

"Only thee to find, the Brahmins—went to the ten regions forth,
"Chaunting to their holy measures—but the words that I had taught.
"Then that Brahmin wise, Parnada—such the name he bears, O king,
"Thee in Kosala, the palace—of king Rituparna saw.
"There to thee, my words addressed he—answer there from thee received.
"I this subtle wile imagined—king of men, to bring thee here.
"Since, beside thyself, no mortal—in the world, within the day,
"Could drive on the fleetest coursers—for a hundred Yojanas.
"To attest this truth, O monarch!—thus I touch thy sacred feet;
"Even in heart have I committed—never evil thought 'gainst thee.
"He through all the world that wanders—witness the all-seeing wind,
"Let him now of life bereave me—if in this 'gainst thee I've sinned:
"And the sun that moveth ever—over all the world, on high,
"Let him now of life bereave me—if in this 'gainst thee I've sinned.
"Witness, too, the moon that permeates—every being's inmost thought;
"Let her too of life bereave me—if in this 'gainst thee I've sinned.
"These three gods are they that govern—these three worlds, so let them speak;
"This my sacred truth attest they—or this day abandon me."

Thus adjured, a solemn witness—spake the wind from out the air;
"She hath done or thought no evil—Nala, 'tis the truth we speak:
"King, the treasure of her virtue—well hath Damayanti kept,
"We ourselves have seen and watched her—closely for three livelong years.
"This her subtle wile she plotted—only for thy absent sake,
"For beside thyself no mortal—might a hundred Yojans drive.
"Thou hast met with Bhima's daughter—Bhima's daughter meets with thee,
"Cast away all jealous scruple—to thy bosom take thy wife."

Even as thus the wind was speaking—flowers fell showering all around:
And the gods sweet music sounded—on the zephyr floating light.

As on this surpassing wonder—royal Nala stood and gazed,
Of the blameless Damayanti—melted all his jealous doubts.
Then by dust all undefiled—he the heavenly vest put on,
Thought upon the King of Serpents—and his proper form resumed.
In his own proud form her husband—Bhima's royal daughter saw,
Loud she shrieked, the undespised—and embraced the king of men.
Bhima's daughter, too, king Nala—shining glorious as of old,
Clasped unto his heart, and fondled—gently that sweet infant pair.
Then her face upon his bosom—as the lovely princess laid,
In her calm and gentle sorrow—softly sighed the long-eyed queen:
He, that form still mire-defiled—as he clasped with smile serene,
Long the king of men stood silent—in the ecstacy of woe.
All the tale of Damayanti—and of Nala all the tale,
To king Bhima in her transport—told Vidarbha's mother-queen.
Then replied that mighty monarch—"Nala, his ablutions done,
"Thus re-joined to Damayanti—I to-morrow will behold."

VRIHADASVA *spake.*

They the livelong night together—slow related, each to each,
All their wanderings in the forest—and each wild adventure strange.
In king Bhima's royal palace—studying each the other's bliss,
With glad hearts, Vidarbha's princess—and the kingly Nala dwelt.
In their fourth year of divorcement—reunited to his wife,
Richly fraught with every blessing—at the height of joy he stood.
Damayanti too re-wedded—still increasing in her bliss,
Like as the glad earth to water—opens its half-budding fruits,
She of weariness unconscious,—soothed each grief, and full each joy,
Every wish fulfilled, shone brightly—as the night, when high the moon.

BOOK XXV.

WHEN that night was passed and over—Nala, that high-gifted king,
Wedded to Vidarbha's daughter—in fit hour her sire beheld.
Humbly Nala paid his homage—to the father of his queen,
Reverently did Damayanti—pay her homage to her sire.
Him received the royal Bhima—as his son, with highest joy,
Honoured, as became him, nobly :—then consoled that monarch wise
Damayanti, to king Nala—reconciled, the faithful wife.
Royal Nala, all these honours—as his homage meet, received;
And in fitting terms, devotion—to his royal sire declared.
Mighty then, through all the city—ran the wakening sound of joy;
All in every street exulting—at king Nala's safe return.
All the city with their banners—and with garlands decked they forth.
All the royal streets, well watered—and with stainless flowers were strewn;
And from door to door the garlands—of festooning flowers were hung;
And of all the gods the altars—were with fitting rites adorned.
Rituparna heard of Nala—in the form of Vahuka,
Now re-wed, to Damayanti—and the king of men rejoiced.
To the king, before his presence—Nala courteous made excuse,
In his turn Ayodhya's monarch—in like courteous language spake.
He, received thus hospitably—wondering to Nishadha's king,
" Bliss be with thee, reunited—to thy queen:" 'twas thus he said.
" Have I aught offensive ever—done to thee, or said, O king
" Whilst unknown, within my palace—thou wert dwelling, king of men ?

"If designed or undesigning—any single act I've done
"I might wish undone, thy pardon—grant me, I beseech thee, king."

NALA *spake.*

"Not or deed or word discourteous—not the slightest hast thou done;
"Hadst thou, I might not resent it—freely would I pardon all.
"Thou of old, my friend, my kinsman—wert, O sovereign of men,
"From this time henceforth thy friendship—be my glory and my joy.
"Every wish anticipated—pleasantly I dwelt with thee,
"As in mine own royal palace—dwelt I ever, king, in thine.
"My surpassing skill in horses—all is thine that I possess;
"That on thee bestow I gladly—if, O king, it seem thee good."
Nala thus to Rituparna—gave his subtle skill in steeds,
Gladly he received the present—with each regulation meet.
Gifted with that precious knowledge—then Bhángásuri the king,
Home returned to his own city—with another charioteer.
Rituparna thus departed—Nala, then the king of men,
In the city of Kundina—sojourned for no length of time.

BOOK XXVI.

There a month when he had sojourned—of king Bhima taking leave,
Guarded but by few attendants—to Nishadha took his way.
With a single splendid chariot—and with elephants sixteen,
And with fifty armed horsemen—and six hundred men on foot;
Making, as 'twere, earth to tremble—hastening onward, did the king,
Enter awful in his anger—and terrific in his speed.
Then the son of Virasena—to king Pushkara drew near;
"Play we once again," then said he—"much the wealth I have acquired:
"All I have, even Damayanti—every treasure I possess,
"Set I now upon the hazard—Pushkara, thy kingdom thou:
"In the game once more contend we—'tis my settled purpose this,
"Brother, at a single hazard—play we boldly for our lives.
"From another he who treasures—he who mighty realm hath won,
"'Tis esteemed a bounden duty—to play back the counter game.
"If thou shrinkest from the hazard—be our game the strife of swords,
"Meet we in the single combat—all our difference to decide.
"An hereditary kingdom—may by any means be sought,
"Be re-won by any venture—this the maxim of the wise.
"Of two courses set before thee—Pushkara, the option make,
"Or in play to stand the hazard—or in battle stretch the bow."
By Nishadha's lord thus challenged—Pushkara, with smile suppressed,
As secure of easy victory—answered to the lord of earth;
"Oh what joy! abundant treasures—thou hast won, again to play;
"Oh what joy! of Damayanti—now the hard-won prize is mine:

" Oh what joy! again thou livest—with thy consort, mighty armed!
" With the wealth I win bedecked—soon shall Bhima's daughter stand,
" By my side, as by great Indra—stands the Apsara in heaven.
" Still on thee hath dwelt my memory—still I've waited, king, for thee;
" In the play I find no rapture—but 'gainst kinsmen like thyself.
" When this day the round-limbed princess—Damayanti, undespised,
" I shall win, I rest contented—still within mine heart she dwells."

Hearing his contemptuous language—franticly thus pouring forth,
With his sword th' indignant Nala—fain had severed off his head.
But with haughty smile, with anger—glaring in his blood-red eyes,
" Play we now, nor talk we longer—conquered, thou'lt no longer talk."
Then of Pushkara the gaming—and of Nala straight began:
In a single throw by Nala—was the perilous venture gained;
Pushkara, his gold, his jewels—at one hazard all was won!
Pushkara, in play thus conquered—with a smile the king rejoined:
" Mine again is all this kingdom—undisturbed, its foes o'ercome.
" Fallen king! Vidarbha's daughter—by thine eyes may ne'er be seen.
" Thou art now, with all thy household—unto abject slavery sunk.
" Not thyself achieved the conquest—that subdued me heretofore!
" 'Twas achieved by mightier Kali—that thou didst not, fool, perceive.
" Yet my wrath, by him enkindled—will I not 'gainst thee direct;
" Live thou henceforth at thy pleasure—freely I thy life bestow,
" And of thine estate and substance—give I thee thy fitting share.
" Such my pleasure, in thy welfare—hero, do I take delight,
" And mine unabated friendship—never shall from thee depart.
" Pushkara, thou art my brother—may'st thou live an hundred years!"

Nala thus consoled his brother—in his conscious power and strength,
Sent him home to his own city—once embracing, once again.

Pushkara, thus finding comfort—answered to Nishadha's lord,
Answered he to Punyasloka—bowing low with folded hands:
" Everlasting be thy glory! may'st thou live ten thousand years!
" That my life to me thou grantest—and a city for mine home!"
Hospitably entertained—there a month when he had dwelt,
Joyful to his own proud city—Pushkara, with all his kin,
With a well-appointed army—of attendant slaves an host,
Shining like the sun departed,—in his full meridian orb.
Pushkara thus crowned with riches—thus unharmed, when he dismissed,
Entered then his royal city—with surpassing pomp, the king:
As he entered, to his subjects—Nala spake the words of peace,

From the city, from the country—all, with hair erect with joy,
Came, with folded hands addressed him—and the counsellors of state.
" Happy are we now, O monarch—in the city, in the fields,
" Setting forth to do thee homage—as to Indra all the gods."
Then at peace the tranquil city—the first festal gladness o'er,
With a mighty host escorted—Damayanti brought he home.
Damayanti rich in treasures—in her father's blessings rich,
Glad dismissed the mighty-minded—Bhima, fearful in his strength.
With the daughter of Vidarbha—with his children in his joy,
Nala lived, as lives the sovereign—of the gods in Nandana.
Re-ascended thus to glory—he, among the kings of earth,
Ruled his realm in Jambudwipa—thus re-won, with highest fame;
And all holy rites performed he—with devout munificence.

THE DEATH OF YAJNADATTA.

This extract from the Ramayana has been edited by M. Chèzy, with a free translation into French prose by M. Bournouf, a literal version into Latin, and a grammatical commentary and notes by the editor.

Through the arts of one of his wives Kaikéyí, to whom he had made an incautious vow to grant her demand, Dasaratha is obliged to send his victorious son Rama into banishment at the very moment of his marriage with the beautiful Sita. Rama is accompanied in his exile by Lakshmana. The following episode describes the misery and distress of the father, deprived of his favourite son.

THE DEATH OF YAJNADATTA.

SCARCE Rama to the wilderness—had with his younger brother gone,
Abandoned to his deep distress—king Dasaratha sate alone.
Upon his sons to exile driven—when thought that king, as Indra bright,
Darkness came o'er him, as in heaven—when pales th' eclipsed sun his light.
Six days he sate, and mourned and pined—for Rama all that weary time,
At midnight on his wandering mind—rose up his old forgotten crime.
His queen Kausalya, the divine—addressed he, as she rested near:
"Kausalya, if thou wak'st, incline—to thy lord's speech thy ready ear.
Whatever deed, or good or ill—by man, oh blessed queen, is wrought,
Its proper fruit he gathers still—by time to slow perfection brought.
He who the opposing counsel's weight—compares not in his judgment cool,
Or misery or bliss his fate—among the sage is deemed a fool.
As one that quits the Amra bower—the bright Palasa's pride to gain,
Mocked by the promise of its flower—seeks its unripening fruit in vain.
So I the lovely Amra left—for the Palasa's barren bloom,
Through mine own fatal error 'reft—of banished Rama, mourn in gloom.
Kausalya! in my early youth—by my keen arrow at its mark,
Aimed with too sure and deadly truth—was wrought a deed most fell and dark.
At length the evil that I did—hath fallen upon my fatal head,
As when on subtle poison hid—an unsuspecting child hath fed;
Even as that child unwittingly—hath made the poisonous fare his food,
Even so in ignorance by me—was wrought that deed of guilt and blood.
Unwed wert thou in virgin bloom—and I in youth's delicious prime,
The season of the rains had come—that soft and love-enkindling time.

Earth's moisture all absorbed, the sun—through all the world its warmth had
spread,
Turned from the north, its course begun—where haunt the spirits of the
dead!
Gathering o'er all th' horizon's bound—on high the welcome clouds appeared,
Exulting all the birds flew round—cranes, cuckoos, peacocks, flew and veered.
And all down each wide-water'd shore—the troubled, yet still limpid floods,
Over their banks began to pour—as o'er them hung the bursting clouds.
And, saturate with cloud-born dew—the glittering verdant-mantled earth,
The cuckoos and the peacocks flew—disputing as in drunken mirth.
In such a time, so soft, so bland—oh beautiful! I chanced to go,
With quiver, and with bow in hand—where clear Sarayu's waters flow.
If haply to the river's brink—at night the buffalo might stray,
Or elephant, the stream to drink,—intent my savage game to slay,
Then of a water cruise, as slow—it filled, the gurgling sound I heard,
Nought saw I, but the sullen low—of elephant that sound appeared.
The swift well-feathered arrow I—upon the bowstring fitting straight,
Toward the sound the shaft let fly—ah, cruelly deceived by fate!
The winged arrow scarce had flown—and scarce had reached its destined aim,
'Ah me, I'm slain,' a feeble moan—in trembling human accents came.
'Ah whence hath come this fatal shaft—against a poor recluse like me,
'Who shot that bolt with deadly craft—alas! what cruel man is he?
'At the lone midnight had I come—to draw the river's limpid flood,
'And here am struck to death, by whom?—ah whose this wrongful deed of
blood.
'Alas! and in my parent's heart—the old, the blind, and hardly fed,
'In the wild wood, hath pierced the dart—that here hath struck their off-
spring dead.

'Ah, deed most profitless as worst—a deed of wanton useless guilt;
'As though a pupil's hand accurs'd—his holy master's blood had spilt.
'But not mine own untimely fate—it is not that which I deplore,
'My blind, my aged parents state—'tis their distress afflicts me more.
'That sightless pair, for many a day—from me their scanty food have earned,
'What lot is theirs, when I'm away—to the five elements returned?
'Alike all wretched they, as I—ah, whose this triple deed of blood?
'For who the herbs will now supply—the roots, the fruit, their blameless food?'
My troubled soul, that plaintive moan—no sooner heard, so faint and low,
Trembled to look on what I'd done—fell from my shuddering hand my bow.
Swift I rushed up, I saw him there—heart-pierced, and fall'n the stream beside,
That hermit boy with knotted hair—his clothing was the black deer's hide.
On me most piteous turned his look—his wounded breast could scarce respire,
And these the words, oh queen, he spoke—as to consume me in his ire:
'What wrong, oh Kshatriya, have I done—to be thy deathful arrow's aim,
'The forest's solitary son—to draw the limpid stream I came.
'Both wretched and both blind they lie—in the wild wood all destitute,
'My parents, listening anxiously—to hear my home-returning foot.
'By this, thy fatal shaft, this one—three miserable victims fall,
'The sire, the mother, and the son—ah why? and unoffending all.
'How vain my father's life austere—the Veda's studied page how vain,
'He knew not with prophetic fear—his son would fall untimely slain.
'But had he known, to one as he—so weak, so blind, 'twere bootless all,
'No tree can save another tree—by the sharp hatchet marked to fall.
'But to my father's dwelling haste—oh Raghu's son, lest in his ire,
'Thy head with burning curse he blast—as the dry forest tree the fire.
'Thee to my father's lone retreat—will quickly lead yon onward path,
'Oh haste, his pardon to entreat—or ere he curse thee in his wrath.

'Yet first, that gently I may die—draw forth the barbed steel from hence,
'Allay thy fears, no Brahmin I—not thine of Brahmin blood the offence.
'My sire, a Brahmin hermit he—my mother was of Sudra race.'
So spake the wounded boy, on me—while turned his unreproaching face.
As from his palpitating breast—I gently drew the mortal dart,
He saw me trembling stand, and blest—that boy's pure spirit seemed to part.
As died that holy hermit's son—from me my glory seemed to go,
With troubled mind I stood, cast down—t' inevitable endless woe.
That shaft that seemed his life to burn—like serpent venom, thus drawn out,
I, taking up his fallen urn—t' his father's dwelling took my route.
There miserable, blind, and old—of their sole helpmate thus forlorn,
His parents did these eyes behold—like two sad birds with pinions shorn.
Of him in fond discourse they sate—lone, thinking only of their son,
For his return so long, so late—impatient, oh by me undone.
My footsteps' sound he seemed to know—and thus the aged hermit said,
'Oh, Yajnadatta, why so slow?—haste, let the cooling draught be shed.
'Long, on the river's pleasant brink—hast thou been sporting in thy joy,
'Thy mother's fainting spirits sink—in fear for thee, but thou, my boy,
'If aught to grieve thy gentle heart—thy mother or thy sire do wrong,
'Bear with us, nor when next we part—on the slow way thus linger long.
'The feet of those that cannot move—of those that cannot see the eye,
'Our spirits live but in thy love—Oh wherefore, dearest, no reply?'
My throat thick swollen with bursting tears—my power of speech that seemed to choke,
With hands above my head, my fears—breaking my quivering voice, I spoke;
'The Kshatriya Dasaratha I—Oh hermit sage, 'tis not thy son!
'Most holy ones, unknowingly—a deed of awful guilt I've done.
'With bow in hand I took my way—along Sarayu's pleasant brink,

'The savage buffalo to slay—or elephant come down to drink.
'A sound came murmuring to my ear—'twas of the urn that slowly filled,
'I deemed some savage wild-beast near—my erring shaft thy son had killed.
'A feeble groan I heard, his breast—was pierced by that dire arrow keen:
'All trembling to the spot I pressed—lo there thy hermit boy was seen.
'Flew to the sound my arrow, meant—the wandering elephant to slay,
'Toward the river brink it went—and there thy son expiring lay.
'The fatal shaft when forth I drew—to heaven his parting spirit soared,
'Dying he only thought of you—long, long, your lonely lot deplored.
'Thus ignorantly did I slay—your child beloved, Oh hermit sage!
'Turn thou on me, whose fated day—is come, thy all-consuming rage.'
He heard my dreadful tale at length—he stood all lifeless, motionless;
Then deep he groaned, and gathering strength—me his meek suppliant did address.
'Kshatriya, 'tis well that thou hast turned—thy deed of murder to rehearse,
'Else over all thy land had burned—the fire of my wide-wasting curse.
'If with premeditated crime—the unoffending blood thou'dst spilt,
'The Thunderer on his throne sublime—had shaken at such tremendous 'guilt.
'Against the anchorite's sacred head—hadst, knowing, aimed thy shaft ac-'cursed,
'In th' holy Vedas deeply read—thy skull in seven wide rents had burst.
'But since, unwitting, thou hast wrought—that deed of death, thou livest 'still,
'Oh son of Raghu, from thy thought—dismiss all dread of instant ill.
'Oh lead me to that doleful spot—where my poor boy expiring lay,
'Beneath the shaft thy fell hand shot—of my blind age, the staff, the stay.
'On the cold earth 'twere yet a joy—to touch my perished child again,

'(So long if I may live) my boy—in one last fond embrace to strain.
'His body all bedewed with gore—his locks in loose disorder thrown,
'Let me, let her but touch once more—to the dread realm of Yama gone.'
Then to that fatal place I brought—alone that miserable pair;
His sightless hands, and hers I taught—to touch their boy that slumbered there.
Nor sooner did they feel him lie—on the moist herbage coldly thrown,
Both with a shrill and feeble cry—upon the body cast them down.
The mother as she lay and groaned—addressed her boy with quivering tongue,
And like a heifer sadly moaned—just plundered of her new-dropped young:
'Was not thy mother once, my son—than life itself more dear to thee?
'Why the long way hast thou begun—without one gentle word to me.
'One last embrace, and then, beloved—upon thy lonely journey go!
'Alas! with anger art thou moved—that not a word thou wilt bestow?'
The miserable father now—with gentle touch each cold limb pressed,
And to the dead his words of woe—as to his living son, addressed:
'I too, my son, am I not here?—thy sire with thy sad mother stands;
'Awake, arise, my child, draw near—and clasp each neck with loving hands.
'Who now, 'neath the dark wood by night—a pious reader shall be heard?
'Whose honied voice my ear delight—with th' holy Veda's living word?
'The evening prayer, th' ablution done—the fire adored with worship meet,
'Who now shall soothe like thee, my son—with fondling hand, my aged feet?
'And who the herb, the wholesome root—or wild fruit from the wood shall 'bring?
'To us the blind, the destitute—with helpless hunger perishing?
'Thy blind old mother, heaven-resigned—within our hermit-dwelling lone,
'How shall I tend, myself as blind—now all my strength of life is gone!

'Oh stay, my child, Oh part not yet—to Yama's dwelling go not now,
'To-morrow forth we all will set—thy mother, and myself, and thou:
'For both, in grief for thee, and both—so helpless, ere another day,
'From this dark world, but little loath—shall we depart, death's easy prey!
'And I myself, by Yama's seat—companion of thy darksome way,
'The guerdon to thy virtues meet—from that great Judge of men will pray.
'Because, my boy, in innocence—by wicked deed thou hast been slain,
'Rise, where the heroes dwell, who thence—ne'er stoop to this dark world
'again.
'Those that to earth return no more—the sense-subdued, the hermits wise,
'Priests their sage masters that adore—to their eternal seats arise.
'Those that have studied to the last—the Veda's, the Vedanga's page,
'Where saintly kings of earth have passed—Nahusa and Yayâti sage;
'The sires of holy families—the true to wedlock's sacred vow;
'And those that cattle, gold, or rice—or lands with liberal hands bestow;
'That ope th' asylum to th' oppressed—that ever love, and speak the truth,
'Up to the dwellings of the blest—th' eternal, soar thou, best loved youth.
'For none of such a holy race—within the lowest seat may dwell;
'But that will be his fatal place—by whom my only offspring fell.'

So groaning deep, that wretched pair—the hermit and his wife, essayed
The meet ablution to prepare—their hands their last faint effort made.
Divine, with glorious body bright—in splendid car of heaven elate,
Before them stood their son in light—and thus consoled their helpless state:
'Meed of my duteous filial care—I've reached the wished for realms of joy;
'And ye, in those glad realms, prepare—to meet full soon your dear-loved
'boy.
'My parents, weep no more for me—yon warrior monarch slew me not,
'My death was thus ordained to be;—predestined was the shaft he shot.'

O

Thus, as he spoke, the anchorite's son—soared up the glowing heaven afar,
In air his heavenly body shone—while stood he in his gorgeous car.
But they, of that lost boy so dear—the last ablution meetly made,
Thus spoke to me that holy seer—with folded hands above his head.
'Albeit by thy unknowing dart—my blameless boy untimely fell,
'A curse I lay upon thy heart—whose fearful pain I know too well.
'As sorrowing for my son I bow—and yield up my unwilling breath,
'So, sorrowing for thy son shalt thou—at life's last close repose in death.'
That curse, dread sounding in mine ear—to mine own city forth I set,
Nor long survived that hermit seer—to mourn his child in lone regret.
This day that Brahmin curse fulfilled—hath fallen on my devoted head,
In anguish for my parted child—have all my sinking spirits fled.
No more my darkened eyes can see—my clouded memory is o'ercast,
Dark Yama's heralds summon me—to his deep, dreary, realm to haste.
Mine eye no more my Rama sees—and grief o'erburns, my spirits sink,
As the swoln stream sweeps down the trees—that grow upon the crumbling
brink.
Oh, felt I Rama's touch, or spake—one word his home-returning voice,
Again to life should I awake—as quaffing nectar draughts rejoice,
But what so sad could e'er have been—celestial partner of my heart,
Than, Rama's beauteous face unseen,—from life untimely to depart.
His exile in the forest o'er—him home returned to Oudes high town,
Oh happy those, that see once more—like Indra from the sky come down.
No mortal men, but gods I deem—moonlike, before whose wondering sight,
My Rama's glorious face shall beam—from the dark forest bursting bright.
Happy that gaze on Rama's face—with beauteous teeth and smile of love,
Like the blue lotus in its grace—and like the starry king above.
Like to the full autumnal moon—and like the lotus in its bloom,

That youth who sees returning soon—how blest shall be that mortal's doom.
Dwelling on that sweet memory—on his last bed the monarch lay,
And slowly, softly, seemed to die—as fades the moon at dawn away.
"Ah, Rama! ah, my son!" thus said—or scarcely said, the king of men,
His gentle hapless spirit fled—in sorrow for his Rama then,
The shepherd of his people old—at midnight on his bed of death,
The tale of his son's exile told—and breathed away his dying breath.

EXTRACTS FROM THE MAHABHARATA.

THE BRAHMIN'S LAMENT.

The hostility of the kindred races of Pandu and Kuru forms one of the great circles of Indian fable. It fills great part of the immense poem, the Mahabhárata. At this period the five sons of Pandu and their mother Kunti have been driven into the wilderness from the court of their uncle Dritarashtra at Nâgapur. The brothers, during their residence in the forest, have an encounter with a terrible giant, Hidimba, the prototype of the Cyclops of Homer, and of the whole race of giants of northern origin, who, after amusing our ancestors, children of larger growth, descended to our nurseries, from whence they are now well-nigh exploded. After this adventure the brothers take up their residence in the city of Ekachara, where they are hospitably received in the house of a Brahmin. The neighbourhood of this city is haunted by another terrible giant, Baka, whose cannibal appetite has been glutted by a succession of meaner victims. It is now come to the Brahmin's turn to furnish the fatal banquet; they overhear the following complaint of their host, whose family, consisting of himself, his wife, a grown up daughter, and a son a little child, must surrender one to become the horrible repast of the monster. In turn, the father, the mother, in what may be fairly called three singularly pathetic Indian elegies, enforce each their claim to the privilege of suffering for the rest.

THE BRAHMIN'S LAMENT.

ALAS for life, so vain, so weary—in this changing world below,
Ever-teeming root of sorrow—still dependent, full of woe!
Still to life clings strong affliction—life that's one long suffering all,
Whoso lives must bear his sorrow—soon or late that must befall.

Oh to find a place of refuge—in this dire extremity,
For my wife, my son, my daughter—and myself what hope may be?
Oft I've said to thee, my dearest—Priestess, that thou knowest well,
But my word thou never heededst—let us go where peace may dwell.
"Here I had my birth, my nurture—still my sire is living here;
"Oh unwise!" 'twas thus thou answeredst—to my oft-repeated prayer.
Thine old father went to heaven—slept thy mother by his side,
Then thy near and dear relations—why delight'st thou here t' abide?
Fondly loving still thy kindred—thine old home thou would'st not leave,
Of thy kindred death deprived thee—in thy griefs I could but grieve.
Now to me is death approaching—never victim will I give,
From mine house, like some base craven—and myself consent to live.
Thee with righteous soul, the gentle—ever like a mother deemed,
A sweet friend the gods have given me—aye my choicest wealth esteem'd.
From thy parents thee, consenting—mistress of my house I took,
Thee I chose, and thee I honoured—as enjoins the holy book.
Thou the high-born, thou the virtuous!—my dear children's mother thou,
Only to prolong my being—thee the good, the blameless, now,

Can I to thy death surrender—mine own true, my faithful wife?
  Yet my son can I abandon—in his early bloom of life,
Offer him in his sweet childhood—with no down his cheek to shade?
  Her, whom Brahma, the all-bounteous—for a lovely bride hath made,
Mother of a race of heroes—a heaven-winning race may make;
Of myself begot, the virgin—could I ever her forsake?
Towards a son the hearts of fathers—some have thought, are deepest moved,
Others deem the daughter dearer—both alike I've ever loved:
She that sons, that heaven hath in her—sons whose offerings heaven may win,
Can I render up my daughter—blameless, undefiled by sin?
If myself I offer, sorrow—in the next world my lot must be,
Hardly then could live my children—and my wife bereft of me.
One of these so dear to offer—to the wise, were sin, were shame,
Yet without me they must perish—how to 'scape the sin, the blame!
Woe! Oh woe! where find I refuge—for myself, for mine, oh where!
Better 'twere to die together—for to live I cannot bear.

The BRAHMIN'S WIFE *speaks.*

As of lowly caste, my husband—yield not thus thy soul to woe,
This is not a time for wailing—who the Vedas knows must know:
Fate inevitable orders—all must yield to death in turn,
Hence the doom, th' irrevocable—it beseems not thee to mourn.
Man hath wife, and son, and daughter—for the joy of his own heart,
Wherefore wisely check thy sorrow—it is I must hence depart.
'Tis the wife's most holy duty—law on earth without repeal,
That her life she offer freely—when demands her husband's weal.
And e'en now, a deed so noble—hath its meed of pride and bliss,
In the next world life eternal—and unending fame in this.

'Tis a high, yet certain duty—that my life I thus resign,
'Tis thy right, as thy advantage—both the willing deed enjoin—
All for which a wife is wedded—long erenow through me thou'st won,
Blooming son and gentle daughter—that my debt is paid and done.
Thou may'st well support our children—gently guard, when I am gone,
I shall have no power to guard them—nor support them, left alone.
Oh, despoiled of thy assistance—lord of me, and all I have,
How these little ones from ruin—how my hapless self to save:
Widow'd, reft of thee, and helpless—with two children in their youth,
How maintain my son, and daughter—in the path of right and truth.
From the lustful, from the haughty—how shall I our child protect,
When they seek thy blameless daughter—by a father's awe unchecked.
As the birds in numbers swarming—gather o'er the earth-strewn corn,
Thus the men round some sad widow—of her noble lord forlorn.
Thus by all the rude and reckless—with profane desires pursued,
How shall I the path still follow—loved and honoured by the good.
This thy dear, thy only daughter—this pure maiden innocent,
How to teach the way of goodness—where her sire, her fathers went.
How can I instil the virtues—in the bosom of our child,
Helpless and beset on all sides—as thou would'st in duty skilled.
Round thy unprotected daughter—Sudras like to holy lore,
Scorning me in their wild passion—will unworthy suitors pour.
And if I refuse to give her—mindful of thy virtuous course,
As the storks the rice of offering—they will bear her off by force.
Should I see my son degenerate—like his noble sire no more,
In the power of the unworthy—the sweet daughter that I bore;
And myself, the world's scorn, wandering—so as scarce myself to know,
Of proud men the scoff, the outcast—I should die of shame and woe.

P

And bereft of me, my children—and without thy aid to cherish,
As the fish when water fails them—both would miserably perish.
Thus of all the three is ruin—the inevitable lot,
Desolate of thee, their guardian—wherefore, Oh, forsake us not!
The dark way before her husband—'tis a wife's first bliss to go,
'Tis a wife's that hath borne children—this the wise, the holy know.
For thee forsaken be my daughter—let my son forsaken be,
I for thee forsook my kindred—and forsake my life for thee.
More than offering 'tis, than penance—liberal gift or sacrifice,
When a wife, thus clearly summoned—for her husband's welfare dies.
That which now to do I hasten—all the highest duty feel,
For thy bliss, for thy well-doing—thine and all thy race's weal.
Men, they say, but pray for children—riches, or a generous friend,
To assist them in misfortune—and a wife for the same end.
The whole race (the wise declare it)—thou the increaser of thy race,
Than the single self less precious—ever holds a second place.
Let me then discharge the duty—and preserve thyself by me,
Give me thine assent, all-honoured—and my children's guardian be.
Women must be spared from slaughter—this the learn'd in duty say,
Even the giant knows that duty—me he will not dare to slay.
Of the man the death is certain—of the woman yet in doubt,
Wherefore, noblest, on the instant—as the victim send me out.
I have lived with many blessings—I have well fulfilled my part,
I have given thee beauteous offspring—death hath nought t' appal mine heart.
I've borne children, I am aged—in my soul I've all revolved,
And with spirit strong to serve thee—I am steadfast and resolved.
Offering me, all-honoured husband—thou another wife wilt find,

And to her wilt do thy duty—gentle as to me, and kind.
Many wives if he espouses—man incurs nor sin nor blame,
For a wife to wed another—'tis inexpiable shame.
This well weighed within thy spirit—and the sin thyself to die,
Save thyself, thy race, thy children—be the single victim I.

Hearing thus his wife, the husband—fondly clasp'd her to his breast,
And their tears they poured together—by their mutual grief oppressed.

THIRD SONG.

Of these two the troubled language—in the chamber as she heard,
Lost herself in grief the daughter—thus took up the doleful word.

The DAUGHTER *spake.*

Why to sorrow thus abandoned?—weep not thus, as all forlorn,
Hear ye now my speech, my parents—and your sorrows may be borne.
Me with right ye may abandon—none that right in doubt will call,
Yield up her that best is yielded—I alone may save you all.
Wherefore wishes man for children?—they in need mine help will be:
Lo, the time is come, my parents—in your need find help in me.
Ever here the son by offering—or hereafter doth atone,
Either way is he th' atoner—hence the wise have named him son.
Daughters too, the great forefathers—of a noble race desire,
And I now shall prove their wisdom—saving thus from death my sire.

Lo, my brother but an infant!—to the other world goest thou,
In a little time we perish—who may dare to question how?
But if first depart to heaven—he that after me was born,
Cease our race's sacred offerings—our offended sires would mourn.
Without father, without mother—of my brother too bereft,
I shall die, unused to sorrow—yet to deepest sorrow left.
But thyself, my sire! my mother—and my gentle brother save,
And their meet, unfailing offerings—shall our fathers' spirits have.
A second self the son, a friend the wife—the daughter's but a grief,
From thy grief thy daughter offering—thou of right wilt find relief.
Desolate and unprotected—ever wandering here and there,
Shall I quickly be, my father!—reft of thy paternal care!
But wert thou through me, my father—and thy race from peril freed,
Noble fruit should I have borne thee—having done this single deed.
But if thou from hence departing—leav'st me, noblest, to my fate,
Down I sink to bitterest misery—save, Oh save me from that state!
For mine own sake, and for virtue's—for our noble race's sake,
Yield up her who best is yielded—me thine own life's ransom make.
Instantly this step, the only—the inevitable take.
Hath the world a fate more wretched—than when thou to heaven art fled,
Like a dog to wander begging—and subsist on others' bread.
But my father, thus preserving—thus preserving all that's thine,
I shall then become immortal—and partake of bliss divine,
And the gods, and our forefathers—all will hail the prudent choice,
Still will have the water offerings—that their holy spirits rejoice.

As they heard her lamentation—in their troubled anguish deep,
Wept the father, wept the mother—'gan the daughter too to weep.

Then the little son beheld them—and their doleful moan he heard;
And with both his eyes wide open—lisped he thus his broken word.
" Weep not father, weep not mother—Oh my sister, weep not so!"
First to one, and then to th' other—smiling went he to and fro.
Then a blade of spear-grass lifting—thus in bolder glee he said,
" With this spear-grass will I kill him—this man-eating giant dead."
Though o'erpowered by bitterest sorrow—as they heard their prattling boy,
Stole into the parents' bosoms—mute and inèxpressive joy.

THE DELUGE.

The following extract from the Mahábhárata was published by Bopp, with a German translation, (the promised Latin version has not yet reached this country,) with four other extracts from the same poem. It is inserted here not on account of its poetical merit, but on account of the interest of the subject. It is the genuine, and probably the earliest, version of the Indian tradition of the Flood. The author has made the following observations on this subject in the Quarterly Review, which he ventures here to transcribe.

Nothing has thrown so much discredit on oriental studies, particularly on the valuable Asiatic Researches, as the fixed determination to find the whole of the Mosaic history in the remoter regions of the East. It was not to be expected that, when the new world of oriental literature was suddenly disclosed, the first attempts to explore would be always guided by cool and dispassionate criticism. Even Sir W. Jones was led away, at times, by the ardour of his imagination; and the gorgeous palaces of the Mahabadian dynasty, which were built on the authority of the Desatir and the Dabistan, and thrown upward into an age anterior even to the earliest Indian civilisation, have melted away, and 'left not a wreck behind,' before the cooler and more profound investigations of Mr. Erskine[a]. Sir W. Jones was succeeded by Wilford, a man of most excursive imagination, bred in the school of Bryant, who, even if he had himself been more deeply versed in the ancient language, would have been an unsafe guide. But Wilford, it is well known, unfortunately betrayed to the crafty and mercenary pundits whom he employed, the objects which he hoped to find; and these unscrupulous interpreters, unwilling to disappoint their employer, had little difficulty in discovering, or forging, or interpolating, whatever might suit his purpose. The honest candour with which Wilford, a man of the strictest integrity, made the open and humiliating confession of the deceptions which had been practised upon him, ought for ever to preserve his memory from disrespect. The fictions to which he had given currency, only retained, and still we are ashamed to say retain, their ground in histories of the Bible and works of a certain school of theology, from which no criticism can exorcise an error once established: still, however, with sensible men, a kind of suspicion was thrown over the study itself; and the cool and sagacious researches of men, probably

[a] See the very valuable papers of this gentleman in the Bombay Transactions.

better acquainted witb their own language tban some of the Brabmins tbemselves, were implicated in the fate of tbe fantastic and, though profoundly learned, ever injudicious reveries of Wilford.

Now, however, tbat we may depend on the genuineness of our documents, it is curious to examine tbe Indian version or versions of the universal tradition of the Deluge; for, besides tbis extract from the Mabábhárata, Sir W. Jones bad extracted from tbe Bhagavata Purana another, and, in some respects, very different legend. Both of tbese versions are strongly impregnated witb the mythological extravagance of India; but the Purana, one of the Talmudic books of Indian tradition, as M. Bopp observes, is evidently of a much later date than the ruder and simpler fable of the old Epic. It belongs to a less ancient school of poetry, and a less ancient system of religion. While it is much more exuberant in its fiction, it nevertheless betrays a sort of apprehension lest it shall shock the less easy faith of a more incredulous reader; it is manifestly from the religious scbool of the followers of Visbnu, and, indeed, seems to have some reference to one of the philosophic systems. Yet tbe outline of the story is the same. In the Máhábbaratic version, Manu, like Noab, stands alone in an age of universal depravity. His virtues, however, are of the Indian cast—the most severe and excruciating penances by which he extorts, as it were, the favour of the deity [b].

[b] The editor remarks, that the name Manuja, Man-born, as the appellative of the human race, is derived from Manu, as likewise Mánawas, *masc.* Man—Mánawi, *fem.* Woman: from thence the Gothic *Mann*, which we have preserved. Manu is thus the representative of Man.

THE DELUGE.

VIVASWATA'S son, a raja—and a sage of mighty fame,
King of men, the first great fathers—in his glory equalled he,
In his might and kingly power—Manu, and in earthly bliss,
And in wonder-working penance—sire and grandsire far surpassed.
With his arms on high out-stretching—wrought the sovereign of men,
Steadily on one foot standing—penance rigorous and dread,
With his downward head low-drooping—with his fixed, unwavering eyes,
Dreed he thus his awful penance—many a long and weary year.
To the penitent with tresses—streaming loose, and wet, and long,
By the margin of Wirini—thus the fish began to speak:
"Blessed! lo, the least of fishes—of the mighty fish in dread,
"Wilt thou not from death preserve me—thou that all thy vows fulfill'st?
"Since the strongest of the fishes—persecute the weaker still,
"Over us impends for ever—our inevitable fate.
"Ere I sink, if thou wilt free me—from th' extremity of dread,
"Meet return can I compensate—when the holy deed is done."
Speaking thus the fish when heard he—full of pity all his heart,
In his hand that fish king Manu—son of Vivaswata took.
Brought the son of Vivaswata—to the river shore the fish,
Cast it in a crystal vessel—like the moonshine clear and bright.
"Rapid grew that fish, O raja—tended with such duteous care,
"Cleaved to him the heart of Manu—as to a beloved son.
"Time rolled on, and larger, larger—ever waxed that wonderous fish,
"Nor within that crystal vessel—found he longer space to move.

Spake again the fish to Manu—as he saw him, thus he spake:
"O all prosperous! O all gentle!—bring me to another place."
Then the fish from out the vessel—blessed Manu took again;
And with gentle speed he bare him,—Manu, to a spacious lake.
There the conqueror of cities,—mighty Manu, cast him in.
Still he grew, that fish so wondrous—many a circling round of years.
Three miles long that lake expanded—and a single mile its breadth,
Yet that fish with eyes like lotus—there no longer might endure;
Nor, O sovereign of the Vaisyas!—might that lake his bulk contain.
Spake again that fish to Manu—as he saw him, thus he spake:
"Bring me now, O blest and holy!—to the Ganga, ocean's bride,
"Let me dwell in her wide waters—yet, O loved one, as thou wilt,
"Be it so; whate'er thy bidding,—murmur would beseem me ill,
"Since through thee, O blest and blameless!—to this wondrous bulk I've grown."
Thus addressed, the happy Manu—took again the fish, and bore
To the sacred stream of Ganga—and himself he cast him in.
Still it grew, as time rolled onward—tamer of thy foes! that fish.
Spake again that fish to Manu—as he saw him, thus he spake:
"Mightiest! I can dwell no longer—here in Ganga's narrow stream;
"Best of men! once more befriend me—bear me to the ocean swift."
Manu's self from Ganga's water—took again that wondrous fish,
And he brought him to the ocean,—with his own hand cast him in.
Brought by Manu to the ocean—very large that fish appeared,
But not yet of form unmeasured,—spread delicious odours round.
But that fish by kingly Manu—cast into the ocean wide,
In these words again bespake him—and he smiled as thus he spake:
"Blessed! thou hast still preserved me—still my every wish fulfilled,

"When the awful time approaches—hear from me what thou must do.
"In a little time, O blessed!—all this firm and seated earth,
"All that moves upon its surface—shall a deluge sweep away.
"Near it comes, of all creation—the ablution day is near;
"Therefore what I now forewarn thee—may thy highest weal secure.
"All the fixed and all the moving—all that stirs, or stirreth not,
"Lo, of all the time approaches—the tremendous time of doom.
"Build thyself a ship, O Manu—strong, with cables well prepared,
"And thyself, with the seven Sages—mighty Manu enter in.
"All the living seeds of all things—by the Brahmins named of yore,
"Place thou first within thy vessel—well secured, divided well.
"From thy ship keep watch, O hermit—watch for me, as I draw near;
"Horned shall I swim before thee—by my horn thou'lt know me well.
"This the work thou must accomplish,—I depart; so fare thee well—
"Over those tumultuous waters—none without mine aid can sail.
"Doubt thou not, O lofty minded!—of my warning speech the truth."
To the fish thus answered Manu—"All that thou requir'st, I'll do."
Thus they parted, of each other—mutual leave when they had ta'en,
Manu, raja! to accomplish—all to him the fish had said.
Taking first the seeds of all things—launched he forth upon the sea;
On the billowy sea, the prudent—in a beauteous vessel rode.
Manu of the fish bethought him;—conscious of his thought the fish,
Conqueror of hostile cities!—with his horn came floating by.
King of men, the born of Manu!—Manu saw the sea-borne fish,
In his form foreshewn, the horned—like a mountain huge and high.
To the fish's head his cable, Manu bound—O king of men!
Strong and firm his cable wound he—round and round on either horn:
And the fish, all conquering raja!—with that twisted cable bound,

With the utmost speed that vessel—dragged along the ocean tide.
In his bark along the ocean—boldly went the king of men:
Dancing with the tumbling billows—dashing through the roaring spray,
Tossed about by winds tumultuous—in the vast and heaving sea,
Like a trembling, drunken woman—reeled that ship, O king of men.
Earth was seen no more, no region—nor the intermediate space;
All around a waste of water—water all, and air and sky.
In the whole world of creation—princely son of Bharata!
None was seen but those seven Sages—Manu only, and the fish.
Years on years, and still unwearied—drew that fish the bark along,
Till at length it came, where lifted—Himavan its loftiest peak.
There at length it came, and smiling—thus the fish addressed the sage:
"To the peak of Himalaya—bind thou now thy stately ship."
At the fish's mandate quickly—to the peak of Himavan
Bound the sage his bark, and ever—to this day that loftiest peak,
Bears the name of Manubandhan—from the binding of the bark.
To the sage, the god of mercy—thus with fixed look bespake:
"I am lord of all creation—Brahma, higher than all height;
"I in fishlike form have saved thee—Manu, in the perilous hour;
"But from thee new tribes of creatures—gods, asuras, men must spring.
"All the worlds must be created—all that moves or moveth not,
"By an all-surpassing penance—this great work must be achieved.
"Through my mercy, thy creation—to confusion ne'er shall run,"
Spake the fish, and on the instant—to the invisible he passed.
Vivaswata's son, all eager—the creation to begin,
Stood amid his work confounded:—mighty penance wrought he then.
So fulfilled that rigorous penance—instant Manu 'gan create—
Instant every living creature—Raja! he began to form.

Such the old, the famous legend—named the story of the Fish,
Which to thee I have related—this for all our sins atones.
He that hears it, Manu's legend,—in the full possession he,
Of all things complete and perfect—to the heavenly world ascends.

NOTES ON NALA.

p. 3. l. 4. *Over, over all exalted.*] This repetition is in the original.

p. 3. l. 5. *Holy deep-read in the Vedas.*] All the perfections, which, according to the opinions and laws of the Hindus, distinguish the sovereign from the rest of mankind, are here ascribed to the hero of the poem. The study of the Vedas must be cultivated by the three superior castes, and ensures both temporal and eternal beatitude. In the laws of Menu it is said, "Greatness is not conferred by years, not by grey hairs, not by wealth, not by powerful kindred." The divine sages have established this rule—Whoever has read the Vedas and their Angas, he is among us great. (JONES's MENU, ii. 254). Of all these duties, answered Bhrigu, the principal is to acquire from the Upanishads a true knowledge of the one supreme God: that is the most exalted of all sciences, because it ensures immortality. (xii. 85). For in the knowledge and adoration of one God, which the Veda teaches, all the rules of good conduct beforementioned in order, are fully comprised. (ib. 87.)

The study of the Vedas is considered the peculiar duty of kings. (vii. 43). The Upanishadas are doctrinal extracts of the Vedas.

The Indian law demands in the most rigorous manner from every one of noble birth, the mastery over the *senses.* Menu says, c. ii. 93, "A man by the attachment of his organs to sensual pleasure, incurs certain guilt; but having wholly subdued them, he thence attains heavenly bliss. v. 94. Desire is never satisfied with the enjoyment of desired objects; as the fire is not appeased with clarified butter; it only blazes more vehemently. v. 97. To a man contaminated by sensuality, neither the Vedas, nor liberality, nor sacrifices, nor strict observances, nor pious austerities, ever procure felicity." The control over every kind of sensual indulgence is enjoined upon the king. vii. 44. Day and night must he strenuously exert himself to gain complete victory over his own organs; since that king alone whose organs are completely subdued, can keep his people firm to their duty.

Skill in the management of horses and chariots, which in a subsequent part of the poem is of great importance to Nala, is often mentioned as a praiseworthy accomplishment of kings. In the Ramayana, for instance, in the description of king Dasaratha, which likewise contains the above-mentioned traits of character—"In this city Ayodhya was a king named Dusharuthâ, descended from Ikshwaku, perfectly skilled in the Veda and Vedangas, prescient, of great ability, beloved by all his people, a great charioteer, constant in sacrifice, eminent in sacred duties, a royal sage, nearly equalling a

Muhurshi, famed throughout the three worlds, mighty, triumphant over his enemies, observant of justice, having a perfect command of his appetites." CAREY and MARSHMAN's translation, sect. vi. p. 64.

p. 3. l. 5. —*in Nishadha lord of earth.*] I have accented this word not quite correctly Nīshădhă, in order to harmonise with the trochaic flow of my metre. It appears to be the same as Nishadha-râshtra and Nishădha-dēsa. See Wilford's list of mountains, rivers, countries; from the Purânas and other books. Asiatic Researches, vol. viii. BOPP.

p. 3. l. 6. *Loving dice, of truth unblemished.*] The Sanscrit word Akshapujah is differently interpreted. Kosegarten renders it in a good sense as "fearing heaven." He argues that it is the poet's object in this passage to describe the good qualities of Nala, and that he does not become a gamester till possessed by the demon Kali. Bopp gives the sense in the text, which seems to connect it with the history of king Yudishtir, to whom it is addressed.

p. 3. l. 7. *Sense subdued.*] The highest notion of this favourite perfection of Indian character, may be given in the words of the author of the Bhagavat-Gita: "The highest perfection to which the soul can attain, is action without passion. The mind is to be entirely independent of external objects; to preserve its undisturbed serenity it should have the conscious power of withdrawing all its senses within itself, as the tortoise draws all its limbs beneath its shell." Action is necessary, but action must produce no emotion—no sensation on the calm spirit within; whatever may be their consequences, however important, however awful, events are to be unfelt, and almost unperceived by the impassive mind; and on this principle Arjuna is to execute the fated slaughter upon his kindred without the least feeling of sorrow or compunction being permitted to intrude on the divine apathy of his soul. Some of the images in which this passionless tranquillity of the spirit is described, appear singularly beautiful:

> As to th' unrais'd unswelling ocean flow the multitudinous streams,
> So to the soul serene, unmov'd—flow in the undisturbing lusts.

And then again the soul, in this state of unbroken quietude,

> Floats like the lotus on the lake, unmov'd, unruffled by the tide.

p. 3. l. 8. *Best, a present Manu he.*] Manu, or Menu, the representative of the human race; the holy, mythological ancestor of the Hindus. In the Diluvium, the Indian version of the Deluge, (see the latter part of this volume), Manu is the survivor of the human race—the second ancestor of mankind. The first Menu is named

"Swayambhuva, or sprung from the self-existing." From him "came six descendants, other Menus, or perfectly understanding the Scripture, each giving birth to a race of his own, all exalted in dignity, eminent in power." Laws of Menu, i. 61. The great code of law "the Hindus firmly believe to have been promulged in the beginning of time by Menu, son or grandson of Brahma, or in plain English the first of created beings, and not the oldest only but the noblest of legislators." Sir W. JONES's preface to Laws of Menu; Works, vii. 76. In the Ramayana, in like manner, king Dasaratha is compared to the ancient king, Menu. The word Manu, as the name of the ancestor of men, is derived from the Sanscrit root Man, to know (WILSON in voce); in the same manner as the Sanscrit Manishá, knowledge, Manushya, Man—as also the Latin Mens, and the German Mensch. According to this etymology, Man, Mensch, properly means "the knowing," the Being endowed with knowledge. The German word, Meinen, to mean, or be of opinion, belongs to the same stock.

p. 3. l. 9. *So there dwelt in high Vidarbha.*] This city is called by our poet Vidarbha Nagara, the city of Vidarbha, and Cundina. According to Wilford it is Burra Nag-poor. BOPP. Colebrooke, Asiatic Researches, remarks, that some suppose it to be the modern Berar, which borders on the mountain Vindhya or Gondwanah. The kingdom of Vidarbha, and its capital Kundini, are mentioned in the very remarkable drama Malati and Madhava. WILSON's Hindu Theatre, ii. 16; and extract from Harivansa, in LANGLOIS Monumens de l'Inde, p. 54.

p. 3. l. 9. *Bhima, terrible in strength.*] Bhima-parâkrama. There is a play upon the words, Bhima meaning terrible.

p. 3. l. 11. *Many a holy act, on offspring.*] He made offerings and performed penance, by which blessings were forced from the reluctant gods. In India not only temporal, but eternal happiness, depends on having children. The son alone by the offering of the Sraddha, or libation for the dead, can obtain rest for the departed spirit of the father. Hence the begetting of a son is a religious duty, particularly for a Brahmin, and is one of the three debts to which he is bound during life. After he has read the Vedas in the form prescribed by Law, has legally begotten a son, and has performed sacrifices to the best of his power, he has paid his three debts, and may then apply his heart to eternal bliss. MENU, vi. 36. By a son a man obtains victory over all people; by a son's son he enjoys immortality; and afterwards, by the son of that grandson, he reaches the solar abode. MENU, ix. 137.

This last passage is immediately followed by the explanation of the Sanscrit word Puttra, son, by "the deliverer from hell." Since the son (trayatè) delivers his father from the hell, named put, he was therefore called puttra by Brahma himself. This explanation, which is given by the Indian etymologists, appears nevertheless, as is often the case, rather forced; since the final syllable, tra, which is translated by deliver (or preserve, WILSON, in voce) is a common ending of many words, without the peculiar signification of delivering: as with this final syllable on the word Pu, to be pure, is formed the noun Puwitra, pure. WILKINS, Grammar, p. 454; KOSEGARTEN. The affix with which this last is formed however, is not tra, but itra, and it affords therefore no ground of objection to the usual etymology of Puttra. WILSON.

The Indian poetry is full of instances of this strong desire for offspring. In the Ramayana, king Dasaratha performs the Aswamedha, or offering of a horse, to obtain a son. "To this magnanimous king, acquainted in every duty, pre-eminent in virtue, and performing sacred austerities for the sake of obtaining children, there was no son to perpetuate his family. At length in the anxious mind of this noble one the thought arose, 'Why do I not perform an Ushwamedha to obtain a son.'" CAREY and MARSHMAN's translation, sect. viii. p. 74. Compare the Raghu Vansa, canto i., and all that is done by king Dilipa to obtain a son: and the poem of the death of Hidimbha, published by Bopp.

p. 3. l. 14. —*in his hospitable hall.*] Hospitality to a Brahmin is of course one of the greatest virtues. "A Brahmin coming as a guest, and not received with just honour, takes to himself all the reward of the housekeeper's former virtue, even though he had been so temperate as to live on the gleanings of harvests, and so pious as to make oblations in five distinct fires." Sir W. JONES, Menu, iii. 100.

p. 3. l. 22. —*as around great Indra's queen.*] Sachi.

> Sachi, soft as morning light,
> Blithe Sachi, from her lord Indrani hight.—Sir W. JONES's Hymn to Indra.

p. 4. l. 2. *Mid her handmaids, like the lightning.*] There are two words of similar signification in the original; one of them implies life-giving. Lightning in India being the forerunner of the rainy season, is looked on as an object of delight as much as terror. BOPP, from the Scholiast.

p. 4. l. 2. —*shone she with her faultless form.*] Sri, or Lakshmi, the goddess of beauty and abundance, at once the Ceres and the Alma Venus of India.

> Daughter of ocean and primeval night,
> Who fed with moonbeams dropping silent dew,
> And cradled in a wild wave dancing light.—Sir W. JONES's Ode to Lacshmi.

p. 4. l. 4. —*never mid the Yaksha race.*] The Yakshas are demigods attendant on

Kuvera, the god of wealth, descendants of Kasyapa by his wife Khasa. They inhabit mountains, and have intercourse with the Apsarasas, or heavenly nymphs. Sometimes they appear not altogether as good beings, sometimes entirely harmless. "The souls of men enslaved to their passions will rise no higher than the Yakshas." Menu, xii. 47. The subject of the Meghaduta, or Cloud-Messenger of Kalidása, so elegantly translated by Mr. Wilson, is the regret of a Yaksha for his beloved wife. Compare Mr. Wilson's note on the Yakshas, Cloud Messenger, p. 69.

p. 4. l. 7. *Nala too, 'mong kings the tiger.*] Nara Sardula, the Tiger warrior. I have retained the literal meaning, though, according to Bopp, it means *in fine compositi, Optimus, præstantissimus.* Mr. Southey's Young Tlalala, in Madoc, is the "tiger of the war."

p. 4. l. 8. *Like Kandarpa in his beauty.*] Kandarpa is the god of love. Kama, Love, or Kam Deo, God of Love. Dipaka, the Inflamer. Manmatha, Heart-disturber. Ananga, the Incorporeal.

God of each lovely sight, each lovely sound.
Soul-kindling, world-inflaming, star y-crowned,
Eternal Camal or doth Smara bright,
Or proud Ananga give thee more delight.—Sir W. Jones, *Ode to Camdeo.*

p. 4. l. 12. *Thus of each, O son of Kunti.*] Kunti was the mother of King Yudishtir, to whom the poem is related. I have usually omitted this address, which is sometimes made to Yudishthir under the title of Bhárata, i. e. descendant of Bharata, or other appellations.

p. 4. l. 15. *There the swans he saw disporting.*] In the original this is a far less poetic bird, and the author must crave forgiveness for having turned his geese into swans. If, however, we are to believe Bohlen, in his learned work, Das Alte Indien, the translators are altogether mistaken; they have been misled by the similarity of the word Hansa to Gans—a goose. The original, he asserts, to mean a mythic bird, closely resembling the swan, or perhaps the tall and brilliant flamingo, which Southey has introduced with such effect in one of his rich descriptions in the Curse of Kehama. The goose, however, according to the general opinion, is so common in Indian mythology, that this must be received with much caution. In the modern Tamulic version of the story, translated by Mr. Kindersley, are substituted, "Milk white Aunnays, descending from the skies, like an undulating garland of pearls." The Aunnays are supposed to be a sort of birds of paradise. They are represented as milk white; remarkable for the gracefulness of their walk; and endowed with considerable gifts.

R

Mr. Wilson, in his Meghaduta, has given me a precedent for the change of geese into swans; see p. 27, v. 71, with the note. And Mr. Ellis, Asiatic Researches, vol. xiv. p. 29, has the following note on the subject: "There are three distinctions of Hamsa; the Raja-hamsa, with a milk-white body and deep red beak and legs, this is the Phenicopteros, or flamingo; the Mallicáesha-hamsa, with brownish beak and legs; and the Dhartarashtra-hamsa, with black beak and legs: the latter is the European swan, the former a variety. The gait of an elegant woman is compared by the Hindu poets to the proud bearing of a swan in the water. Sonnerat, making a mistake similar to that in the text, translates a passage in which this allusion occurs, in words to the following purport, 'Her gait resembled that of a goose.' Other writers have fallen into the same error." The swans, ou Plutôt les Génies ailès, play the same part in an extract from the Harivansa, translated by M. Langlois, in his Monumens Littéraires de l'Inde, *Paris*, 1827, p. 158. The first part of the Harivansa has just appeared, under the auspices of the Oriental Translation Committee.

p. 5. l. 4. *Like the Aswinas in beauty.*] See Asiatic Researches, i. 263; ix. 323. Ramayana, i. 226.

p. 5. l. 7. *Gandharvas.*] Celestial choristers, of beautiful forms and complexion, usually seen in Hindu sculptures attendant on the deities.

Celestial genii tow'rd their king advance
(So called by men) in heaven Gandharvas named,
For matchless music famed.
Soon when the bands in lucid rows assemble,
Flutes breathe, and citherns tremble.

Sir W. Jones, Ode to Indra.—See Ramayana, I. 125.

p. 5. l. 7. *the Serpents.*] The serpents are objects of reverence and veneration in India. They are called Naga, not going; Uragas—breast-going. Their residence is in Pátála, though they are occasional visitants both of heaven and earth. See notes to book V. In the Bhagavat Gita, Arjun sees Brahma "sitting on his lotus-throne; all the Reshees and Ooragas (serpents)," Wilkins' translation, p. 91. According to Wilson, (Sanscrit Dict. voce Naga), the race of these beings is said to have sprung from Kadru, the wife of Kasyapa, in order to people Pátála, or the regions below the earth.

p. 5. l. 7. *The Rakshasas.*] Demons who assume at will the forms of lions, tigers, horses, and other animals, as well as the human shape, with numerous heads and arms. They are represented as cannibals who devour their enemies. See Ramayana.

p. 6. l. 6. —*and with passion heart-possessed.*] It is, literally, her mind (or thought), being possessed by the *heart-sleeper*, (i. e. love, reposing or dwelling in the heart). WILSON.

p. 6. l. 8. *The Swayembara.*] The self-election. The princesses in India enjoyed this singular privilege. The festival was proclaimed, and from the assembled suitors the lady selected her future husband. The Swayembara is not among the eight kinds of marriages mentioned in the third book of Menu, as customary among the higher castes, in which the parents in general arrange such contracts. The provision in the ninth book (v. 90), appears to belong to the lower classes.—"Three years let a damsel wait, though she be marriageable; but after that term let her choose for herself a bridegroom of equal rank." In the Raghuvansa, a poem, parts of which the author of this translation, if he could command leisure to make himself better acquainted with Sanscrit, would consider well worthy of being introduced to the English reader, there is a very remarkable and beautiful book, describing a Swayembara. This is likewise held at Vidarbha by the daughter of the king. The Mahabharat also describes the Swayembara of the princess Draupadi.

p. 6. l. 17. *The lord of many peasants.*] Vaisya, the third caste, husbandmen and traders.

p. 6. l. 22. *All with rich and various garlands.*] The use of garlands in the decoration of the houses and temples of the Hindus, and of flowers in their offerings and festivals, furnishes employment to a particular tribe or caste, the málácáras, or wreath makers. WILSON, note 57, on Meghaduta or Cloud-messenger.

p. 7. l. 2. *Indra's world.*] Indra is the God of heaven, of the thunder and lightning, storm and rain: his dwelling is sometimes placed on mount Meru, as the heaven of the Greeks on Olympus. His city is called Amaravati; his palace Vaijayanti; his garden Nandana. (KOSEGARTEN.)

Hail, mountain of delight,
Palace of glory, bless'd by glory's king.
With prospering shade embower me, whilst I sing
Thy wonders yet unreached by mortal flight.
Sky-piercing mountain! in thy bowers of love,
No tears are seen, save where medicinal stalks
Weep drops balsamic o'er the silvered walks.
No plaints are heard, save where the restless dove
Of coy repulse, and mild reluctance talks.

Mantled in woven gold, with gems inchas'd,
With emerald hillocks graced,
From whose fresh laps, in young fantastic mazes,
Soft crystal bounds and blazes,
Bathing the lithe convolvulus, that winds
Obsequious, and each flaunting arbour binds. SIR W. JONES, Ode to Indra.

p. 7. l. 3. *Narada and Parvata.*] Two of the divine Munis or Rishis. Narada is the son of Brahma; a friend of Krishna, a celebrated lawgiver, and inventor of the vinà, or lute. (WILSON, Dict. in voce.) Narada is mentioned as one of the "ten lords of created beings, eminent in holiness." MENU, i. 34, 35.

p. 7. l. 4. *In full trust is thine.*] Bopp connects '*visrabdha*' with '*pranaya*,' and renders them *speratas nuptias*. I should rather join it adverbially with '*sarvam*, all;' that is, 'yours in full trust or confidence: grant me your affection.' There is something indelicate, though inartificial, in Damayanti's urging matrimony so earnestly. WILSON.

p. 7. l. 5. *Them salutes the cloud-compeller.*] 'Maghavan' is by some explained 'the cloudy.' I have adopted the word used by the translators of Homer.

p. 7. l. 12. *Theirs this everlasting kingdom.*] Kshetriyas, or warriors, slain in battle, are transported to Swerga, the heaven of Indra, by the Apsarasas or nymphs of heaven: hence they are his "ever-honoured guests." "Those rulers of the earth, who, desirous of defeating each other, exert their utmost strength in battle, without ever averting their faces, ascend after death directly to heaven." MENU, vii. 89. Indra means to say, "Why are none new-killed in battle now-a-days, that I see none arriving in my heaven, Swerga?"

p. 7. l. 12. *—even as Kamadhuk is mine.*] Kamadhuk, the cow of plenty. She was brought forth on churning the ocean to produce the amrita, or drink of immortality. The interpretation is doubtful; it may be that this realm is to them the cow of plenty, (as bestowing upon them all their wishes), as the cow of plenty is mine. See BOPP's and KOSEGARTEN's notes.

p. 7. l. 15. *Thus addressed by holy Sakra.*] Sakra, a name of Indra.

Hail, Dyapeter, dismay to Bala's pride,
Or speaks Purander best thy martial fame,
Or Sacra, mystic name.—SIR W. JONES, Hymn to Indra.

Bala and Vritra were the "giants" slain by Indra.

p. 7. l. 23. *As they spake, the world-protectors.*] The world-protectors are the eight gods next below the trine supreme, Brahma, Siva, and Vishnu. They are Indra, the god of heaven; Surya, the god of the sun; Soma or Chandra, the god of the moon; Agni, the god of fire; Pavana, the god of the wind; Kuvera, the god of wealth; Varuna, the god of water; Yama, the god of the infernal regions. At present four only of these gods are introduced; Indra, Yama, Agni, and Varuna. Compare, however, Mr. Wilson's note to Vikrama and Urvasi, Hindu Theatre, i. 219.

p. 8. l. 8. —*equal to the god of love.*] Manmatha, a name of Kandarpa, or Camdeo, the god of love.

p. 11. l. 2. *Pledge me to thy faith, O raja.*] Bopp has rendered '*pranayaswa,*' *uxorem duc*, but this is questionable. The root '*ni,*' with the preposition '*pari,*' has that sense, but with '*pra*' its usual acceptation is 'to love, to bear affection.' I have not met with it in the sense 'to marry.' Bopp is followed by Rosen in assigning this sense to '*prani.*' Wilson.

p. 11. l. 8. —*the vile noose will I endure.*] Hanging was not considered by the Hindus an undignified mode of self-destruction. See Hindu Theatre, ii. 237 and 299.

p. 11. l. 17. *He, who all the world compressing.*] Nala here recites the separate pretensions and attributes of the great deities, first, of Hutasa, a name of Agni, the god of fire. The sense here is extremely obscure. Bopp renders it literally. 'Qui hanc terram totam contraxit,' seems ambiguous. It may refer to the agency of fire in compacting the world and again consuming it, or simply shrivelling it up, while in the act of consuming.

p. 11. l. 19. *He, in awe of whose dread sceptre.*] Yama: he is called the Dharma raja, king of justice. Wilford in Asiatic Researches. Compare Southey's description in the Curse of Kehama, Canto xxii., with the note from Wilford on which it is founded; and his interview with Sawitri in Bopp's collection of Extracts from the Mahábhárata.

p. 11. l. 21. —*slayer of the infernal host.*] Indra. He was the conqueror of the Danavas or dæmons:

When through the waves of war thy charger sprang,
Each rock rebellowed, and each forest rang,
The vanquish'd Asurs felt avenging pains. SIR W. JONES, Ode to Indra.

p. 11. l. 23. —*in thy mind if thou couldst choose.*] (At the close full stop misprinted for comma). Varuna, the god of waters. Schlegel and Rosen consider that a sloka, describing the attributes of Varuna, has been lost—that in this line 'varanam, seligendum' should be written instead of 'Varunam.' The Calcutta edition has the same reading, however, and the change is not necessary: if any alteration be made it should probably be in the first word, and 'Vriyatám' be read in place of 'Kriyatám.' WILSON.

p. 14. l. 1. *Came the day of happy omen.*] The Indians, like all other Asiatic nations, have their fortunate and unfortunate days. The month is divided into thirty lunar days (tithis), which are personified as nymphs. See the Dissertation on the lunar year by Sir W. JONES, Asiatic Researches, iii. 257. In the Laws of Menu are multifarious directions concerning the days of the moon fit or unfit for particular actions. "The dark lunar day destroys the spiritual teacher; the fourteenth destroys the learner; the eighth and the day of the full moon destroy all remembrance of Scripture; for which reason he must avoid reading on those lunar days."

p. 14. l. 5. *They, the court with golden columns, etc.*] The literal rendering is, 'they entered the hall (the stage, or place of exhibition, a spacious court or quadrangle) splendid with columns of gold, and brilliant with a portal; a temporary or triumphal arch (torana).' There is allusion to such a porch or portal in the Mudrá Rakshasa (Hindu Theatre, ii. 181, 182), also in the Toy Cart, (i. 82). For gold pillars see CRAWFURD's description of the Hall of Audience at Ava.

"The roof is supported by a great number of pillars: with the exception of about fourteen or fifteen inches at the bottom of each pillar, painted of a bright red, the whole interior of the palace is one blaze of gilding—although little reconcileable to our notions of good taste in architecture, the building is unquestionably most splendid and brilliant, and I doubt whether so singular and imposing a royal edifice exists in any other country." *Embassy to Ava*, 133. WILSON.

p. 14. l. 10. —*delicate in shape and hue.*] Bopp's text is 'ákáravantah suslakshnab, having forms and delicate.' The Calcutta edition reads 'ákáraverna suslakshnah, elegant in figure and colour (complexion). Delicacy of colour, i. e. a lighter shade, scarcely amounting to blackness at all, is in general a mark of high caste. WILSON.

p. 14. l. 13. *As with serpents, Bhogavati.*] Bhogavati, the capital of the serpents in the infernal world. In the Ramayana, Ayodhya is described as guarded by warriors, as Bhogavati by the serpents.

p. 15. l. 22. *Nala's form might not discern.*] The form of the gods, as it is here strikingly described by the poet, differs from that of men by the absence of those defects which constitute the inferiority of a mortal body to that of the inhabitants of the Indian heaven. The immortal body does not perspire, it is unsoiled by dust, the garlands which they wear stand erect, that is, the flowers are still blooming and fresh. The gods are further distinguished by their strong fixed gaze, and by floating on the earth without touching it. They have no shadow. Nala's form is the opposite of all these. KOSEGARTEN.

p. 15. l. 23. *—saw she, and with moveless eyes.*] "The gods are supposed to be exempt from the momentary elevation and depression of the upper eyelid, to which mortals are subject. Hence a deity is called 'Animisha' or 'Animesha,' one whose eyes do not twinkle." Mr. Wilson, in his note to Vikrama and Urvasi, (Hindu Theatre, i. 237. p. 60.), quotes this passage, and suggests that the "marble eyes of Venus, by which Helen knew the goddess, and which the commentators and translators seem to be much perplexed with, are probably the 'stabdha lochana,' the fixed eyes of the Hindus, full and unveiled for an instant, like the eyes of a marble statue. Mr. Wilson has, I think, been misled by the words ὄμματα μαρμαίροντα, which rather expresses the contrary. Μαρμαίρω is to glitter, and is applied in many places in Homer to the gleaming of armour. The μαρμαρυγὰς θηεῖτο ποδῶν of the Odyssey is well translated by Gray, "glance their many-twinkling feet." In Mr. Wilson's curious reference to Heliodorus (the passage is in the Æthiopica, iii. 13.) the author appears to write from Egyptian rather than Grecian notions. He extorts, somewhat violently, a meaning from Homer's words, δεινὼ δέ οἱ ὄσσε φάανθην, which they by no means necessarily bear; but the analogy is as curious if Egyptian as if Grecian.

p. 15. l. 25. *On his shadow, garland drooping.*] According to the Zoroastrian religion, one of the distinctions of human beings after the restoration of all things and the final triumph of Ormuzd, shall be that they shall cast no shadow; μήτε σκίαν ποιοῦντας. THEOPOMP. apud Plut. de Isid. et Osirid. Compare ANQUETIL DU PERRON and KLEUKER, Anhang zum Zendavesta, i. 140.

p. 16. l. 14. *And the happy pair devoutly.*] The devotion of the silent spirit, the purely mental worship, is the holiest and most acceptable service to the gods. Compare WILKINS, Bhagavat-Gita, p. 74; MENU, ii. 85; vi. 235.

p. 16. l. 19. *Agni gave his own bright presence.*] Agni gave him the command of fire whenever he willed. Hutása is a name of Agni; hut-asa, 'qui sacrificium edit,' i. e. ignis. Bopp's explanation, 'mundos per Deum Agnem splendentes,' has been adopted as giving the clearest sense. Varuna gave the command of water.

p. 16. l. 23. —*each his double blessing gave.*] Bopp translates this, 'par liberorum dederunt,' but the original says, 'all (or each) gave a pair,' i. e. a couple of blessings; making eight, as stated above; each of the four gods giving two. WILSON.

p. 17. l. 4. *Lived in bliss, as with his Sachi.*] Indra, the giant-killer; Sachi, his spouse.

p. 17. l. 7. *Of the horse the famous offering.*] The reader will be best acquainted with the Aswamedha, or sacrifice of the horse, from the spirit and felicity with which it has been introduced by Southey in the Curse of Kehama. See also the Ramayana.

p. 18. l. 2. *As they parted thence, with Kali.*] Dwapara and Kali are the names of the third and fourth ages of the world. The latter is here personified as a male deity.

p. 18. l. 17. —*the Puranas too the fifth.*] In the original 'Akhyana, history, legend.' The four Vedas are the Rig-veda, the Yajur Veda, the Sama Veda, and the Atharvana. Akhyana is, as it were, tradition superadded to scripture.

p. 20. l. 5. *Nala in the dusky twilight, etc.*] This is rather an unmanageable passage; but the Latin translation has not rendered its purport correctly. 'Upaspris' can in no case mean 'calcare:' it implies touching, and especially touching or sipping water, as part of the ceremony of purification. As Menu; "Let each man sprinkle the cavities of his body, and taste water in due form, etc." In the text of this passage, 'upaspris' is used for touching or sprinkling. In others, it is used in the sense of ablution, bathing. In the lexicons it is explained 'upasparsa sparsamátre, snánáchamanayorapi, touch in general, ablution, sipping water.' In the Mitákshara, on the subject of personal purification, the direction is, after evacuations, 'Dwijo nityam upaspriset, Let the man of two births always perform the upaspersa,' i. e. says the commentator, 'áchámet, let him sip water.' The sense of the passage of the text is, 'that Nala sat down to evening prayer; (as Menu directs, he who repeats it sitting at evening twilight, etc.,) after performing his purifications, and sipping water, but without having washed his feet, such ablution being necessary not because they had been soiled, but because such an act is also part of the rite of purification. As the Mitakshara, 'etasmát páda prakshálana prápti, after that purification, comes the washing of the feet,' especially prior to any religious act. So Colebrooke: "Having washed his hands and feet, and having sipped water, the priest sits down to worship." A. R. v. 363. WILSON.

p. 20. l. 12. *In the dice of dice embodied.*] 'Sicut taurus boum:' the literal translation of the phrase is explained by the commentator Nilakantha, as 'talus inter talos eximius.' I have adopted Schlegel's reading, which substitutes Dwapara for Kali, as possessing the dice.

p. 20. l. 23. *Then the charioteer advancing.*] The charioteer appears as one of the great officers of state: the master of the horse would convey as lofty a meaning to an English ear.

p. 21. l. 1. *Ill they brook this dire misfortune.*] Vyasana is a misfortune in a king: neglect of his duty for the pleasures of the chase, gambling, etc.

p. 22. l. 1. *Punyasloka, king of men.*] Punyasloka is a title applied to other kings celebrated in Hindu poetry, to Yudishthir, and also to Vishnu: it means, celebrated in sacred poems. WILSON, Dict. in voce.

p. 23. l. 13. —*to Cundina's city go.*] Cundina is the capital of the kingdom of Vidarbha.

p. 23. l. 23. *Thence departing, to Ayodhya.*] Ayodhya, or Oude, is famous in all the early poetry of India. "On the banks of the Suruyoo is a large country called Koshula, gay and happy, and abounding with cattle, corn, and wealth. In that country was a famous city called Ayodhya, built formerly by Munoo, the lord of men. A great city, twelve yojanas in extent, the houses of which stood in triple and long-extended rows. It was rich, and perpetually adorned with new improvements; the streets and valleys were admirably disposed, and the principal streets well watered. It was filled with merchants of various descriptions, and adorned with abundauce of jewels; difficult of access, filled with spacious houses, beautified with gardens, and groves of mango trees, surrounded by a deep and impassable moat, and completely furnished with arms; was ornamented with stately gates and porticoes, and constantly guarded by archers, etc. etc." Ramayana, translated by CAREY and MARSHMAN, vol. i. p. 60.

p. 25. l. 16. —*to the region of the south.*] Dakshinaptha signifies properly the land on the right hand; as in the Semitic languages the south is that which is on the right land. It means here the land to the south of the Nerbudda. Dakshinapatha is very probably meant in the word used by Arrian, Dachinabades. KOSEGARTEN.

p. 25. l. 17. *Passing by Avanti's city.*] Avanti, which Bopp makes a mountain, according to Kosegarten and Mr. Wilson is a city, Oujein. Bopp draws a somewhat fanciful analogy between Avanti and the Aventine at Rome. He refers also to Himavan, qu. Mavanten, 'montem.' The philological student will do well to consult this note of Bopp. In the Meghadúta, Oujein is Aventi:

> Behold the city, whose immortal fame,
> Glows in Avanti's or Visala's name. line 193.

The synonymes of Oujein are thus enumerated by Hemachandra: Ujjayini, Visála, Avanti, and Pushparacandini. Rikshaván, i. e. bear-having, the mount of bears, is part of the Vindhya chain, separating Malwa from Kandesh and Berar. WILSON.

p. 25. l. 18. *Vindhya here, the mighty mountain.*] See note to 'Cloud-Messenger,' page 92 to 94. Compare likewise Asiatic Researches, i. p. 380, where, in one of the famous inscriptions on the staff of Feroz Shah, it is named as one of the boundaries of Aryaverta, the land of virtue, or India. It is named also in the curious Indian grant of land found at Tanna. Asiatic Researches, i. 366.

p. 25. l. 18. *—and Payoshni's seaward stream.*] Payoshni, a river that flows from the Vindhya, mentioned in the Brahmanda Purana. Asiatic Researches, viii. 341.

p. 25. l. 20. *—this to Cosala away.*] Cosala, a city of Ayodhya, or Oude. Cosala is mentioned in the Brahmanda Purana as beyond the Vindhya mountains. Asiatic Researches, viii. 343.

p. 27. l. 7. *Both together by one garment.*] The poet supposes that Damayanti had bestowed half her single garment upon Nala. BOPP. This, however, does not appear to be the case.

p. 28. l. 4. *From her virtue none dare harm her.*] Spenser's Una, and still more the lady in Comus, will recur to the remembrance of the English reader. See Quarterly Review, vol. xlv. p. 20.

p. 28. l. 24. *—may the genii of the woods.*] He calls on the Adityas, Vasavas, and Rudras, the Aswinas, the Maruts. This is the literal version. They are different orders of genii, each consisting of a definite number. The Adityas are twelve, and preside over the different months. They are called the children of Kasyapa and of Aditi his wife. According to Mr. Wilkins (notes to the Bhagavat-Gita, p. 144), they are no more than emblems of the sun for each month in the year. Mr. Wilkins gives their names:

The Vasavas, or Vasus, are eight. Indra is the first. They are the guardians of the world, and apparently the same with the eight gods mentioned in the early part of the poem.

The Rudras are eleven; according to some the eleven personifications of Siva, who bears the name of Rudra. Bhagavat-Geta, p. 85. note 144. " The lord of creation meditated profoundly on the earth, and created the gods, the Vasus, Rudras, and Adityas." COLEBROOKE, in Asiatic Researches, viii. 453.

For the Aswinas see former note.

The Maruts are forty-nine: they preside over the winds (MENU, iii. 88.) The chief god of the wind, Pavana, is called Marut. Their origin is described in the Ramayana, i. 420. See also the Hindu Pantheon, p. 92.

p. 30. l. 14. *Hence one moment, thus deserted.*] Conjugal duty is carried to a great height in the laws of Menu: " Though unobservant of approved usages, or enamoured of another woman, or devoid of good qualities, yet a husband must constantly be revered as a god by a virtuous wife." v. 154.

p. 31. l. 11.—*in the satyr-haunted wood.*] Swapada, dog-footed: the dog is an unclean animal in India. As the goat-footed, the ' capripedes satyri' in Greece, I have thought the satyr not so exclusively Greek but that it might be used for any " wild man of the woods." The word is also derived from ' swan, a dog,' and ' ápad, to resemble,' and is explained by Mr. Wilson, ferocious, savage.

p. 32. l. 21.—*uttered loud her curse of wrath.*] The power of a curse, according to Indian belief, will be best illustrated to the reader of English poetry by " the Curse of Kehama." In the " Death of Yajnadatta," included in this volume, we find the effects of a Brahmin's curse described.

p. 33. l. 5. *Trees of every form and stature.*] I have omitted a long list of trees, the names of which, conveying no notion to an English ear, and wanting the characteristic epithets of Ovid's or of Spenser's well-known and picturesque forest description, would only perplex the reader with several lines of unintelligible words. To the Indian ear these names, pregnant with pleasing associations, and descriptive in their etymological meaning, would no doubt convey the same delight as those of the Latin or English poet.

p. 33. l. 9. —*serpents, elves, and giants saw.*] Kosegarten has translated this word 'elves:' they are a kind of evil spirit. In Menu, ii. 96, they are named with the Yakshas and Rakshasas as partaking of unclean food.

p. 35. l. 22. *All the trees of richest foliage.*] A general description has again been substituted in these two lines for the names of various trees.

p. 36. l. 4. —*of the regal sacrifice.*] The king's offering. See COLEBROOKE, in Asiatic Researches, viii. 430.

p. 36. l. 15. —*soma quaffing, fire adoring.*] Soma, the juice of the Asclepias acida, the moon plant. Drinking the expressed juice of this plant is a holy ceremony, used at the completion of a sacrifice, and sanctifies the drinker. "He alone is worthy to drink the juice of the moon plant who keeps a provision of grain sufficient to supply those whom the law commands him to nourish, for the term of three years or more. But a twice-born man, who keeps a less provision of grain, yet presumes to taste the juice of the moon plant, shall gather no fruit from that sacrament, even though he taste it at the first or solemn, or much less at any occasional ceremony." MENU, iii. 197. All the ancestors of the Brahmins are 'Soma-pas, moon-plant drinkers.'

p. 36. l. 15. —*fire adoring.*] Watching or maintaining the sacred fire is another duty: it peculiarly belongs to priests and hermits. The latter may watch the fire mentally: "Then having reposited his holy fires, as the law directs, in his mind, let him live without external fire, without a mansion, wholly silent, feeding on roots and fruit." MENU, vi. 25.

p. 37. l. 2. —*sweet as the amrita draught.*] For the amrita, the drink of immortality, see Curse of Kehama, the extract from the Mahábhárata quoted by Mr. Wilkins in his notes to the Bhagavat-Geta, and Ramayana, I. 410.

p. 37. l. 10. *To the ancient famous hermits.*] These famous hermits, whose names I have omitted, were Bhrigu, Atri, and Vasishta,

p. 37. l. 11. *Self-denying, strict in diet.*] The sixth book of Menu is filled with instructions to those who are engaged in 'tapasa:' it is entitled, "On Devotion."

" When the father of a family perceives his muscles become flaccid, and his hair gray, and sees the child of his child, let him then seek refuge in a forest. Abandoning all food eaten in towns, and all his household utensils, let him repair to the lonely wood, committing the care of his wife to her sons, or accompanied by her, if she choose to attend him. Let him take up his consecrated fire, and all his domestic implements of making oblations to it, and departing from the town to the forest, let him dwell in it with complete power over his organs of sense and of action. With many sorts of pure food, such as holy sages used to eat, with green herbs, roots, and fruit, let him perform the five great sacraments before mentioned, introducing them with due ceremonies. Let him wear a black antelope's hide, or a vesture of bark; let him suffer the hairs of his head, his beard, and his nails, to grow continually." MENU, vi. 2. et seqq.

p. 37. l. 18. *pulchris femoribus.*] Clausulam hanc prudens omisi.

p. 37. l. 25. *Take thy seat, they said, oh lady.*] The hospitality of the hermits to Damayanti is strictly according to law. " With presents of water, roots, and fruit, let him honour those who visit his hermitage."

p. 37. l. 27. *In your sacred fires, your worship.*] " Let him, as the law directs, make oblations on the hearth with three sacred fires." MENU, vi. 9. Compare iv. 25.

p. 37. l. 27. *—blameless, with your beasts and birds.*] Hermits were to have "a tender affection for all animated bodies." MENU, vi. 8.

p. 38. l. 12. *—twice-born Sages, know ye me.*] The three first castes are " twice-born." The first birth is from the natural mother; the second from the ligation of the zone; the third from the due performance of the sacrifice: such are the births of him who is usually called twice-born, according to the text of the Veda; among them his divine birth is that which is distinguished by the ligation of the zone and sacrificial cord, and in that birth the Gayatri is his mother, and the Acharya his father. MENU, ii. 169.

p. 39. l. 15. *Through devotion now we see him.*] The kind of prophetic trance, in which holy men, abstracted from all earthly thoughts, were enwrapt, enabled them to see things future.

p. 40. l. 6. *Best of trees, the Asoca blooming.*] The Asoca is a shrub consecrated to Mahadeva; men and women of all classes ought to bathe, on a particular day, in some holy stream, especially the Brahma-putra, and drink water with the buds of the Asoca floating in it. This shrub is planted near the temples of Siva, and grows abundantly on Ceylon. Sita is said to have been confined in a grove of it, while in captivity by Ravana; other relators say that she was confined in a place or house called Asocavan. The Asoca is a plant of the first order of the eighth class, of leguminous fructification, and bears flowers of exquisite beauty. Van Rheede (Hortus Malab. vol. v. tab. 59.) calls it Asjogam. See Asiatic Researches, iii. 254, 277. MOOR, Hindu Pantheon, 55.

p. 40. l. 17. *Truly be thou named Asoca.*] Asoca, from *a*, privative, and *soka*, grief: a play of words, as when Helen, in Euripides, is called ''Ἑλεναϛ, the destroyer of ships.' Many other instances will occur to the classical reader. In Malati and Madhava, the forlorn lover in turn addresses different objects of nature, the clouds, the birds, and the elephants, to inform him whether they have seen his lost mistress. ACT ix. See, however, Mr. WILSON's note, who seems to think that he addresses the sylvan deities.

p. 42. l. 8. —*Manibhadra, guard us well.*] Manibhadra, the tutelar deity of travellers and merchants: probably a name of Kuvera, the god of wealth.

p. 42. l. 11. *To the realm of Chedi's sovereign.*] Chedi is the name of the country now called Chandail. The country is perpetually named in the marriage of Roukmini, extracted from the Harivansa by Mons. LANGLOIS, Monumens de l'Inde, p. 96.

p. 43. Compare the Raghuvansa, ch. v. 43 to 49.

p. 43. l. 12. —*lo, a herd of elephants,*
Oozing moisture from their temples—

> Where the wild elephant delights to shed
> The juice exuding fragrant from his head.
>
> WILSON's Cloud-Messenger, p. 127, and note.

p. 44. l. 7. —*the three worlds seemed all appalled.*] Swerga, heaven, Martya or Bhumi, the earth, and Patala, hell.

p. 44. l. 21. *And Vaisravana the holy.*] Vaisravana is another name of Kuvera, the god of wealth.

p. 45. l. 13. *In some former life committed.*] The soul, in its transmigration, expiates the sins committed in a former state of being. This necessary corollary from the doctrine of the metempsychosis appears to have prevailed among the pharisaic Jews in the time of our Saviour: " Master, who did sin, this man or his parents, that he was born blind." JOHN, ix. 2.

p. 46. l. 15. —*in their curious gamesome play.*] Kutuhalát, rendered by Bopp 'cum voluptate,' means, 'from curiosity.' WILSON.

p. 47. l. 13. *I with but one robe, him naked.*] Bopp's text is incorrect here. Instead of 'Tam. ekavasanam,' the accusative masculine, it should be 'Tam. ekavasaná, I with one garment clad,' the nominative feminine, referring to Damayanti, not to Nala: " I with one garment following him naked and deprived of reason, like one crazed, had not slept for many nights." WILSON.

p. 47. l. 28. *That I eat not broken victuals.*] Among the kinds of food proscribed to a Brahmin are, " the food of a servile man and the orts of another."

p. 47. l. 28. —*wash not feet with menial hand.*] The Latin translation, 'ne faciam pedibus cursum,' is faulty: the sense is, " that I perform not washing of the feet." Damayanti means that she is not to perform menial offices appropriated to persons of low caste. Stipulating for a carriage would be rather extraordinary. WILSON.

p. 49. l. 9. *Nárada, the famous hermit.*] One of the Devarshis, and a great prophet, who is supposed to be still wandering about the world. 'Nara' signifies a thread or clew, a precept, and 'da,' giver. Whenever he appears he is constantly employed in giving good counsel. WILKINS, note on Bhagavat-Geta.

p. 49. l. 23. *Ere the tenth step he had counted—him the sudden serpent bit.*] 'Dasa' means both 'bite' and 'ten.'

p. 50. l. 12. *Neither Brahmin fear, nor Sages.*] In Indian poetry four classes of holy men, or Rishis, are distinguished, and rise, one above the other, in the following rank: Rajarshis, royal Rishis; Maharshis, great Rishis; Brahmarshis, Brahminical Rishis; and Dewarshis, divine Rishis. KOSEGARTEN. Another enumeration specifies seven grades. WILSON, in voce.

p. 50. l. 26. *Saying thus, of vests celestial—gave he to the king a pair.*] The dress of a Hindu consists of two pieces of cloth, one, the lower garment fastened round his waist, and one the upper garment thrown loosely and gracefully over the shoulders. WILSON.

p. 51. l. 6. *In the art of dressing viands.*] This, it will be remembered, was one of the gifts bestowed by the gods on Nala at his marriage.

p. 51. l. 12. *—hundred hundreds is thy pay.*] Suvarnas, a certain measure of gold. Wilson, Dict. ni voce.

p. 52. l. 2. There is in the text a second line, repeating the same sentiment. Bopp proposes to reject the first, I have omitted the second.

p. 53. l. 7. *And a royal grant for maintenance.*] See Bopp's note. I have adopted the second sense of the word Agrahārah. Such grants were not uncommon in India, as throughout the east. See the grants on copper-plates found near Bombay, Asiatic Researches, i. 362. So the well-known gifts of the king of Persia to Themistocles.

p. 53. l. 15. *—on a royal holiday.*] A day proclaimed as fortunate by the king.

p. 54. l. 1. *—like Manmatha's queen divine.*] The bride of Kámadeva is Rati, pleasure.

p. 54. l. 5. *Like the pallid night, when Rahu.*] This is a favourite simile of the Indian poets.

> That snatched my love from the uplifted sword,
> Like the pale moon from Rahu's ravenous jaws.
>
> Wilson's Malati and Madhava, p. 62.

> ——— and now thou fall'st, a prey
> To death, like the full moon to Rahu's jaws
> Consigned. Ibid. p. 115.

In Indian mythology, eclipses are caused by the dragon Rahu attempting to swallow up the moon. The origin of their hostility is given in a passage quoted by Mr. Wilkins from the Mahabharat, in his notes to the Bhagavat-Geta:—"And so it fell out that when the Soors were quenching their thirst for immortality, Rahoo, an Asoor, assumed the form of a Soor, and begun to drink also; and the water had but reached his throat, when the sun and moon, in friendship to the Soors, discovered the deceit, and instantly Narayan cut off his head as he was drinking, with his splendid weapon, chakra. And the gigantic head of the Asoor, emblem of a monstrous summit, being thus separated from his body by the chakra's edge, bounded into the heavens with a dreadful cry, whilst the ponderous trunk fell, cleaving the groud asunder, and shaking the whole earth unto its foundations, with all its islands, rocks, and forests. And from this time the head of Rahoo resolved on eternal enmity, and continueth even unto this day at times to seize upon the sun and moon." p. 149.

p. 54. ls. 4—10. This long train of similes, in which the images of the lotus flower and the moon so perpetually occur, is too characteristic to be omitted or compressed. I have here and there used the license of a paraphrase.

p. 54. l. 15. *To the unadorned a husband.*] "Married women must be honoured and adorned by their fathers and brethren, by their husbands, and by the brethren of their husbands, if they seek abundant prosperity." MENU, iii, 55.

p. 54. l. 22. —*the moon's bride.*] Rohinia. The moon, as in the northern mythologies, is a male deity. See WILFORD, in Asiatic Researches, iii, 384. Rohinia is explained by Mr. Wilson, the fourth lunar asterism, figured by a wheeled carriage, and containing five stars, probably α β γ δ ε, Tauri. In mythology the asterism is personified as one of the daughters of Daksha, and wives of the moon.—Sanscrit Dict. in voce. Comp. Vikrama and Urvasi, p. 57.

p. 57. *Dasarna.*] Dasarna is mentioned in the Cloud Messenger of Kalidasa.

Dasarna's fields await the coming shower.

See likewise Mr. Wilson's note, p. 37.

p. 59. l. 2. *By the wind within the forest—fanned, intensely burns the fire.*] Kosegarten supposes this to mean, that as the incessant wind kindles the fire in the grove of bamboos, so their repeated words may fan the fire of pity in the heart of Nala.

p. 63. l. 9. *To desire this deed unholy.*] A second marriage in a woman is considered in India an inexpiable breach of conjugal fidelity. "A virtuous wife ascends to heaven, though she have no child, if after the decease of her lord she devotes herself to pious austerity. But a widow, who from a wish to bear children, slights her deceased husband by marrying again, brings disgrace on herself here below, and shall be excluded from the seat of her lord." MENU, v, 160-161. "She who neglects her former (purva) lord, though of a lower class, and takes another (para) of a higher, becomes despicable in this world, and is called para purva, or one who had a different husband before." Ibid. 163.

p. 64. l. 4. *With the ten good marks distinguished.*] Avarttas are "locks," curls, or twists of the hair in certain forms on different parts of the body—here they are ap-

T

parently: forehead 1, head 2, chest 2, ribs 2, flanks 2, crupper 1. In the Magha, v. 9, we have the term Avarttina applied to horses; on which the commentator observes, "Avarttina signifies horses having the ten Avarttas, marks of excellence; they are, two on the breast, two on the head, two on the hollows of the ribs, two on the hollows of the flanks, and one on the crupper (Prapata); these are called the ten Avarttas. Avartta means an eddy, or whirlpool, and the name is applied to dispositions of the hair of a horse which resemble a whirlpool." WILSON.

p. 64. l. 4. —*born in Sindhu.*] The Sindhu is the Indian name for the Indus; the neighbouring territory is called Sind. See Asiatic Researches, viii. 336.

p. 65. l. 7. *Matali.*] The charioteer of Indra. See Rhaguvansa, xii, 86, and Sacontala.

p. 66. l. 10. *Ten miles, lo, it lies beyond us.*] A Yojana; according to some eleven, according to others five or six English miles. I have given a round number.

p. 66. l. 12. *Vibhitak.*] 'Beleric Myrobalan.' WILSON, Sanscrit Dict. in voce.

p. 66. l. 21. *Kotis.*] A Koti is ten millions.

p. 68. l. 11. *Kali.*] It must be remembered that Kali, while within the body of Nala, had been enchanted by the serpent Karkotaka.

p. 68. l. 16. Damayanti; who had cursed in the forest all who had caused the misery of Nala.

p. 68. l. 25. Compare Prospero's power in the Tempest.

p. 70. l. 4. *All the region round him echoing—with the thunders of his car.*] This scene rather reminds us of the watchman reporting the rapid approach of Jehu, "The driving is like the driving of Jehu the son of Nimshi; for he driveth furiously." II Kings ix, 20.

p. 70. l. 6. *In their joy they pawed and trampled.*] The horses of Nala had been before conveyed to the city of king Bhima by Varshneya.

p. 70. l. 16. —*as at sound of coming rain.*] The rejoicing of the peacocks at the approach of rain is very sweetly described in the play of Malati and Madhava, translated by Mr. Wilson.

Ah Malati, how can I bear to contemplate
The young Tamala, bowed beneath the weight
Of the light rain; the quivering drops that dance
Before the cooling gale; the joyful cry
That echoes round, as pleased the pea-fowl hail
The bow of heaven propitious to their loves.—p. 108.

In the Cloud Messenger, the Yaksha who addresses the cloud, fears lest it should be delayed by the cry of the peacock—

Or can the peacock's animated hail
The bird with lucid eyes, to lure thee fail.—l. 147.

In another passage,

Pleased on each terrace, dancing with delight,
The friendly peacock hails thy grateful flight.—l. 215.

p. 76. l. 19. —*much and various viands came.*] The reader must remember the various gifts bestowed on king Nala by the gods upon his marriage.

p. 77. l. 22. —*of her mouth ablution made.*] Washing the mouth after food, which Damayanti in her height of emotion does not forget, is a duty strictly enjoined in the Indian law, which so rigidly enforces personal cleanliness. "With a remnant of food in the mouth, or when the Sraddha has recently been eaten, let no man even meditate in his heart on the holy texts." Menu, iv, 109. "Having slumbered, having sneezed, having eaten, having spitten, having told untruths, having drunk water, and going to read sacred books, let him, though pure, wash his mouth." v. 145.

p. 79. l. 17. —*hair dishevelled, mire-defiled.*] As a sign of sorrow and mourning.

p. 80. l. 4. *I will be.*] "I will be," must be the commencement of the prayer uttered by the bridegroom at the time of marriage. It does not correspond with any of those cited by Mr. Colebrooke. It is probably analogous to that given by him, Asiatic Researches, viii, p. 301. Wilson.

p. 81. l. 11. *He through all the world that wanders—witness the all-seeing lord.*] See the curious Law of Ordeal, Asiatic Researches, vol. i, p. 402, "On the trial by fire, let both hands of the accused be rubbed with rice in the husk, and well examined: then let seven leaves of the Aswatha (the religious fig-tree) be placed on them, and bound with seven threads." Thou, O fire, pervadest all beings; O cause of purity, who givest evidence of virtue and of sin, declare the truth in this my hand.

p. 81. l. 27. —*flowers fell showering all around.*] These heavenly beings are ever ready, in the machinery of Hindu epics, to perform their pleasing office (of showering flowers on the head of the happy pair) on every important occasion: they are called Pushpa-vrishti, or flower-rainers. Moor, Hindu Pantheon, 194. See in the Raghu-vansa, ii, 60. No sooner has king Dílípa offered himself to die for the sacred cow o his Brahminical preceptor, than "a shower of flowers" falls upon him.

p. 86. l. 3. —*stands the Apsara in heaven.*] The birth of the Apsarasas is thus related in the Ramayana.

Then from the agitated deep upsprung
The legion of Apsarasas, so named
That to the watery element they owed
Their being. Myriads were they born, and all
In vesture heavenly clad, and heavenly gems;
Yet more divine their native semblance, rich
With all the gifts of grace and youth and beauty.
A train innumerous followed, yet thus fair
Nor god nor demon sought their widowed love;
Thus Rághava they still remain, their charms
The common treasure of the host of heaven.—Wilson's Translation, Preface to the Drama of Vikrama and Urvasi, p. 13.

p. 87. l. 16. *Pushkara appeased.*] The Calcutta edition has a better reading than that of Bopp. Instead of Prasantè Pushkare (Pushkara appeased), it is Prasantè tu pure, (the city being tranquil, the rejoicings having ceased). Wilson.

p. 87. l. 21. *Nala sate, as in Nandana.*] Nandâna is the garden of Indra.

p. 87. l. 23. *Ruled his realm in Jambudwipa.*] Sic in Puranis India nominatur. Bopp.

NOTES TO

THE DEATH OF YAJNADATTA.

p. 91. l. 15. *So I the lovely Amra left.*] The Amra is the Mangifern Indica. This tree is not only valuable in the estimation of the Indians for the excellence of its fruits; the belief that the burning juice of its flowers is used to steep the darts of love, enhances their veneration for this beautiful tree. It is frequently mentioned in their poetry. M. Chezy.

p. 91. l. 15. —*for the Palasa's barren bloom.*] The Palasa is the Butea Frondosa of Koenig. Its flowers, of great beauty, are papilionaceous; and its fruit, entirely without use in domestic economy, compared particularly with the Amra, may well be called barren. M. Chezy. See Sir W. Jones's Essay on the Botany of India; and the Asiatic Researches, vol. iii.

p. 91. l. 19. —*hath fallen upon my fatal head.*] "Yes, iniquity once committed, fails not of producing fruit to him who wrought it; if not in his own person, yet in his son's; or if not in his son's, yet in his grandson's." Menu, iv. 173.

p. 92. l. 2. —*where haunt the spirits of the dead!*] The south; the realm of Yama, the judge of the dead.

p. 92. l. 3. —*on high the welcome clouds appeared.*] The beauty of nature after the rainy season has refreshed the earth, is a favourite topic in Indian poetry. The Cloud Messenger, so gracefully translated by Mr. Wilson, is full of allusions to the grateful progress of the cloud, welcomed as it passes along by the joy of animate and inanimate beings. Quote 61—70, 131—142. Compare, in the Hindu Drama, the Toy Cart, act v.

p. 93. l. 2. *As though a pupil's hand accursed.*] The offences of a pupil against a tutor, almost the holiest relation of life, are described in the Laws of Menu, ii. 191 to 218, 242, 8. "By censuring his preceptor, though justly, he will be born an ass; by falsely defaming him, a dog; by using his goods without leave, a small worm; by envying his merit, a larger insect or reptile." As the Roman law did not contemplate the possibility of parricide, that of Menu has no provision against the crime in the text.

p. 93. l. 6. *—to the five elements returned.*] A common Indian phrase for death. The ether is the fifth element.

p. 93. l. 15. *Kshatriya.*] The second, or warrior-caste. The kings in India were usually of this caste.

p. 93. l. 25. *Raghu.*] One of the famous ancestors of Dasaratha. The poem of the Raghu Vansa has recently appeared, edited by M. Stenzler.

p. 94. l. 3. *My sire, a Brahmin hermit he—my mother was of Sudra race.*] This seems inconsistent with Menu: "A Brahmin, if he take a Sudra to his bed as his first wife, sinks to the regions of torment; if he begets a child by her, he loses even his priestly rank." iii, 17; also 18, 19.

p. 96. l. 14. *The miserable father now.*] See in Menu, the penalties and expiations for killing a Brahmin undesignedly, xi, 74, 82; compare 90. An assaulter of a Brahman with intent to kill, shall remain in hell a hundred years; for actually striking him with like intent, a thousand; as many small pellets of dust as the blood of a Brahmin collects on the ground, for so many thousand years must the shedder of that blood be tormented in hell." xi. 207, 8.

p. 97. l. 23. *I've reached the wished for realms of joy.*] Among the acts which lead to eternal bliss are these: "Studying and comprehending the Veda—showing reverence to a natural or spiritual father." Menu, xii, 83.

NOTES TO

THE BRAHMIN'S LAMENT.

p. 104. l. 5. —*a heaven-winning race may make.*] Literally: Whom Brahma has placed with me in trust for a future husband, and through whose offspring I may obtain with my progenitors the regions secured by ablutions made by a daughter's sons. WILSON.

p. 104. l. 15. A line is omitted here, which seems to want a parallel to make up the sloka. Bopp has omitted it in his translation.

p. 105. l. 21. —*Sudra like.*] The lowest caste who are not privileged, and indeed have no disposition in the native barrenness of their minds to study the sacred Vedas.

p. 105. l. 25. *As the storks the rice of offering.*] We follow Bopp in refining these birds from birds of coarser prey.

THE DESCENT OF THE GANGES.

FIRST PRINTED IN THE QUARTERLY REVIEW, VOL. XLV.

THE descent of the Ganges is the sequel of another fiction still more monstrous, but perhaps one of the most singular of the cosmogonical notions of the ancient Indians. Sagara, the king of Ayodhya (Oude), was without offspring—in almost all eastern countries the most grievous calamity incident to man, more especially to those of noble or royal race. By the most surpassing penances he obtains an oracle from the wise Brighu, predicting that one of his wives will bring forth a single son, the other *sixty thousand!* Accordingly the fair Cesina gives birth to Asamanja; his other wife to a gourd, which, like the egg of Leda, is instinct with life. From the seeds of this gourd, preserved with great care, and fed with ghee, come forth in due time the sixty thousand boys. The son of Cesina was a youth of the most malicious and cruel disposition; his pastime was to throw little infants into the river, and solace himself with their cries. He is sent into exile by his just and humane father, where he has a son, Ansuman, as gentle and popular as Asamanja was malignant and odious. King Sagara prepares to offer the Aswameda, the famous sacrifice of the horse. The holy and untouched steed is led forth, as in the 'Curse of Kehama,' among the admiring multitude, by the youthful Ansuman, when on a sudden a monstrous serpent arises from the earth, and drags it into the abyss. Sagara, in wrath, commands his sixty thousand sons to undertake the recovery of the steed from the malignant demon who has thus interrupted the sacrifice. Having searched long in vain, they begin to dig into the bowels of the earth, until,—

'Cloven with shovel and with hoe, pierced by axes and by spades,
Shrieked the earth in frantic woe; rose from out the yawning shades
Yells of anguish, hideous roars from the expiring brood of hell—
Serpents, giants, and Asoors, in the deep abyss that dwell.
Sixty thousand leagues in length, all unweary, full of wrath,
Through the centre, in their strength, clove they down their hellward path.'

U

The gods, expecting the whole frame of the world, thus undermined, to perish in total ruin, assemble around Brahma to implore his interposition. He informs them that Vishnu, in the form of Kapila, has been the robber of the horse, and that in due time the god will avenge himself. From Patala, the hell of Indian mythology, the Sagaridæ recommence their impious and destructive work.

> 'And downward dug they many a rood, and downward till they saw aghast,
> Where the earth-bearing elephant stood, ev'n like a mountain tall and vast.
> 'Tis he whose head aloft sustains the broad earth's forest-clothed round,
> With all its vast and spreading plains, and many a stately city crown'd.
> If underneath the o'erbearing load bows down his weary head, 'tis then
> The mighty earthquakes are abroad, and shaking down the abodes of men.
> Around earth's pillar moved they slowly, and thus in humble accents blest
> Him the lofty and the holy, that bears the region of the East.
> And southward dug they many a rood, until before their shuddering sight,
> The next earth-bearing elephant stood, huge Mahapadmas' mountain height.
> Upon his head earth's southern bound, all full of wonder, saw they rest.
> Slow and awe-struck paced they round, and him, earth's southern pillar, blest.
> Westward then their work they urge, king Sagara's six myriad race,
> Unto the vast earth's western verge, and there in his appointed place
> The next earth-bearing elephant stood, huge Saumanasa's mountain crest;
> Around they paced in humble mood, and in like courteous phrase addrest,
> And still their weary toil endure, and onward dig until they see
> Last earth-bearing Himapandure, glorying in his majesty.'

At length they reach the place where Vishnu appears in the form of Kapila, with the horse feeding near him; a flame issues forth from the indignant deity, and the six myriad sons of Sagara become a heap of ashes.

The adventure devolves on the youthful Ansuman, who achieves it with perfect success; Vishnu permits him to lead away the steed, but the ashes of his brethren cannot be purified by earthly water; the goddess Ganga must first be brought to earth, and, having undergone lustration from that holy flood, the race of Sagara are to ascend to heaven. Yet a long period elapses; and it is not till the reign of the virtuous Bhagiratha, that Brahma is moved by his surpassing penance to grant the descent of Ganga from heaven. King Bhagiratha had taken his stand on the top of Gokarna, the sacred peak of the Himavan, (the Himalaya,) and here

' Stands with arms outstretch'd on high, amid five blazing fires, the one
Towards each quarter of the sky, the fifth the full meridian sun.
Mid fiercest frosts on snow he slept, the dry and withered leaves his food,
Mid rains his roofless vigil kept, the soul and sense alike subdued.'

His prayers are irresistible; but Brahma forewarns him, that the unbroken descent of Ganga from heaven would be so overpowering, that the earth would be unable to sustain it, and Siva must be propitiated, in order that he may receive on his head the precipitous cataract. Under this wild and unwieldy allegory appears to lurk an obscure allusion to the course of the Ganges among the summits, and under the forests of the Himalaya, which are the locks of Siva.

' High on the top of Himavān the mighty Mashawara stood;
And " Descend," he gave the word to the heaven-meandering water—
Full of wrath, the mandate heard Himavān's majestic daughter.
To a giant's stature soaring and intolerable speed,
From heaven's height down rush'd she pouring upon Siva's sacred head.
Him the goddess thought in scorn with her resistless might to sweep
By her fierce waves o'erborne, down to hell's remotest deep.'

Siva, in his turn enraged, resists her fury.

' Down on Sankara's holy head, down the holy fell, and there
Amid the entangling meshes spread, of his loose and flowing hair,
Vast and boundless as the woods upon the Himalaya's brow,
Nor ever may the struggling floods rush headlong to the earth below.
Opening, egress was not there, amid those winding, long meanders.
Within that labyrinthine hair, for many an age the goddess wanders.'

The king again has recourse to his penances, Siva is propitiated, and the stream by seven[b] channels finds its way to the plains of India. The spirit and the luxuriance of the description which follows, of the king leading the way, and the obedient waters rolling after his car, appear to us of a high order of poetry.

[b] Schlegel supposes the three western streams to be the Indus, which appears under its real name the Sind, the Iaxartes, and the Oxus; are not the Sareswatie, or perhaps the Sutlej, under the name of Sita, and the Jumna meant? Of the eastern branches, it is not difficult to fix the Burhampooter. Schlegel suggests the Irawaddy, and the Blue River of China. Why not the Alacananda and the Gogra? The main stream bears the name of the Bhaghiratha, till it joins the Alacananda and takes the name of the Ganges.

'Up the raja at the sign upon his glittering chariot leaps,
Instant Ganga the divine follows his majestic steps,
From the high heaven burst she forth first on Siva's lofty crown,
Headlong then and prone to earth thundering rushed the cataract down.
Swarms of bright-hued fish came dashing; turtles, dolphins in their mirth,
Fallen or falling, glancing, flashing, to the many gleaming earth.
And all the host of heaven came down, spirits and genii, in amaze,
And each forsook his heavenly throne, upon that glorious scene to gaze.
On cars, like high tower'd cities, seen, with elephants and coursers, rode,
Or on soft swinging palanquin, lay wondering each observant god.
As met in bright divan each god, and flash'd their jewell'd vestures' rays,
The coruscating æther glow'd, as with a hundred suns ablaze.
And with the fish and dolphins gleaming, and scaly crocodiles and snakes,
Glanc'd the air, as when fast streaming the blue lightning shoots and breaks:
And in ten thousand sparkles bright went flashing up the cloudy spray,
The snowy flocking swans less white, within its glittering mists at play.
And headlong now poured down the flood, and now in silver circlets wound,
Then lakelike spread all bright and broad, then gently, gently flowed around,
Then 'neath the cavern'd earth descending, then spouted up the boiling tide,
Then stream with stream harmonious blending, swell bubbling up or smooth subside.
By that heaven-welling water's breast, the genii and the sages stood,
Its sanctifying dews they blest, and plung'd within the lustral flood.
Whoe'er beneath the curse of heaven from that immaculate world had fled,
To th' impure earth in exile driven, to that all-holy baptism sped;
And purified from every sin, to the bright spirit's bliss restor'd,
Th' etherial sphere they entered in, and through th' empyreal mansions soar'd.
The world in solemn jubilee behold these heavenly waves draw near,
From sin and dark pollution free, bathed in the blameless waters clear.
Swift king Bhagiratha drave upon his lofty glittering car,
And swift with her obeisant wave bright Ganga followed him afar.'

THE END.